STREETCORNER RESEARCH

*An Experimental Approach
to the Juvenile Delinquent*

STREETCORNER

1964   CAMBRIDGE, MASSACHUSETTS

RESEARCH

An Experimental Approach
to the Juvenile Delinquent

RALPH SCHWITZGEBEL

HARVARD UNIVERSITY PRESS

Dedicated to Charles W. Slack
and to the boys from whose lives
came the substance of this research

Since a book is never exclusively the result of one person's efforts but, rather, a combination of the author's observations and the insights of teachers, associates, and friends, I hasten to acknowledge my indebtedness to those to whom this book is dedicated—Dr. Charles W. Slack and the boys who served as research subjects. As will be clear from further reading, Dr. Slack's ideas, enthusiasm, and encouragement were essential in the development of the research reported herein. As a student I had long discussions with him that brought light to the dark areas of crime and penology, and which I still gratefully remember. To the boys who participated as subjects, I extend, on behalf of all the experimenters, my sincerest appreciation.

Most of the research reported here was done under the direction of five experimenters: Dr. Slack, formerly Assistant Professor of Clinical Psychology and Research Associate in the Laboratory of Social Relations at Harvard and presently Research Associate in Psychology, Brooklyn College; the Rev. Juan Cortes, S.J., a Spanish priest and graduate student in psychology at Harvard; Mr. Stanley R. Dubinsky, a graduate student in social work at Boston University; Dr. David Kantor, Lecturer on Social Relations at Harvard; and myself. The names of our subjects, as used in this book, are, of course, fictitious and all incidental information that might in any way identify them has been eliminated. However, the biographical data in Appendices A and B, which are related to the research design, are as accurate as possible. The verification of this data, the collection of follow-up data, and the selection of control sub-

jects according to preestablished criteria have been done
by evaluators acting independently of the experimenters,
with the assistance of the Youth Service Board and the
Department of Probation and Parole, Commonwealth of
Massachusetts. This help is very much appreciated, since
without it independent evaluation would have been very
difficult if not impossible.

In Part I of this book, I discuss, in considerable detail,
the delinquency project, Streetcorner Research, describing
its development and the nature of our specific research.
The project, however, was based upon, and leads to, many
theoretical concepts that are considerably broader than
those which can be conveyed by a description of the project
alone. Therefore, in Part II, some of these broader concepts
are discussed, and the observations and research upon
which they are based are presented. It is also pointed out
that, although the results obtained by Streetcorner Research are in some instances quite encouraging, this does
not necessarily mean that the procedures used by our
project should be used by other groups interested in reducing delinquency. It is still too soon to know whether these
procedures will work well under a different set of conditions—as might be found in other cities or in rural areas
or with middle-class delinquents. Some of our procedures
might work better; some might be completely ineffective.
Therefore, they should be used only if their effectiveness is
constantly evaluated.

Many fortunate circumstances have made this research
possible; a special word of acknowledgment is owed
Dr. David C. McClelland, Chairman of the Department
of Social Relations at Harvard, who, over a period of several years, generously allowed the use of the facilities under
his direction and frequently gave us the benefit of his good
judgment and support. In such a setting ideas can be freely

exchanged, while claims and counterclaims must be buttressed by the presentation of tangible results. In addition, I am indebted to many others, among whom I want to mention, in particular, Dr. Marc Fried, Dr. William J. Freeman, and Mrs. Laura Morris for a community-wide view of the problems of behavior; Dr. Milton Greenblatt, Dr. Eliot Danzig, Mr. David A. Kolb, and Mr. George Litwin for demonstrating in their own work the possibility of collaborative research between experimenters and subjects; Dr. Raymond C. Hummel, Dr. Robert Rosenthal, and the late Dr. Samuel Waldfogel for assisting in research design; Dr. James Muller for his ability to combine optimism with diagnostic acumen; and Dr. Erich Lindemann, Dr. Frank R. Ervin, Dr. Winifred S. Lair, Dr. Walter N. Pahnke, and Dr. Brendan A. Maher for their kindly counsel. Also, I have been fortunate to have had the secretarial assistance of Mrs. Doris Simpson, the administrative and financial assistance of my brother, Dr. Robert Schwitzgebel, the valuable philosophical consultation of Mr. Kent E. Armeson, the encouragement of Dr. and Mrs. Conrad Chapman, and the humane and deep social perspectives of my wife, Colleen.

I am especially grateful for the support of the Aaron E. Norman Fund, Inc., the trustees of the estate of the late Mary W. B. Curtis, the Ford Foundation, the Charles Hayden Foundation, and the Louis and Pauline Cowan Foundation, Inc. Without the help of these foundations, the research reported in this book could not have been conducted; and, without an additional grant from the Aaron E. Norman Fund, Inc., this manuscript could not have been written. Finally, for their kind permission to quote material originally appearing in their publications, I want to thank the editors of *Mental Hygiene, Psychoanalysis and the Psychoanalytic Review,* and the *American Journal of Psychiatry;* and the publishers of Teilhard de

Chardin, *The Divine Milieu* (New York: Harper and Row, 1960), Barker and Wright, *The Midwest and Its Children* (Evanston, Ill.: Row, Peterson, 1954), Aichhorn, *Wayward Youth* (New York: Viking, 1935), and Farber and Wilson, eds., *Control of the Mind* (New York: McGraw-Hill, 1961).

Ralph Schwitzgebel

April 21, 1964
Cambridge, Massachusetts

Contents

Part I: The Research

In 1959 Herbert Strean described "The Use of the Patient as Consultant." This therapist, a young student of psycho-analysis, wanted to see to what extent a patient could prescribe his own treatment. His first case was a fourteen-year-old boy who was underachieving in school and wanted "nothin' from nobody." Several therapists had previously attempted to relate to this boy and had failed. In the first interview, Strean asked the boy, "What should I do?" The boy replied that he should be quiet. He told the therapist: "You have to promise to say nothing. I'll be the boss around here." Consequently, the therapist was quiet.

During the next several interviews the boy and therapist merely looked at each other with no comments other than "Hello" and "Goodby." In the middle of the sixth session, the boy commented, "I'm quitting; I don't like it. Nothing is happening. You are no better than the other guys." He then became silent and drew diagrams of electrical circuits which he fantasied he could use to burn down the clinic. He cursed the therapist and the building in monosyllables. When the therapist asked whether the boy could teach him something about electricity, he got up and walked out stating dryly: "You've got a lot to learn. I'll think about coming back and showing you."

For the next several months at each therapy session, the boy taught the therapist about electricity; then, he told the therapist that he was "tired of being the big shot." When the therapist asked, "What should I do?" he was advised "not to get so excited, do less talking, and give with more action." The therapist did "give with more action" by finding the boy a vocational school that taught electrical theory. The boy enrolled in the school, became enthusiastic about his work, and eventually learned how to read and how to develop friendships.

Strean used this experimental approach with several other patients as well and he suggested that "perhaps implicit in the use of the patient as consultant are basic and generic concepts of psychotherapy" (1959, p. 10). This was one of the early uses of an experimental role in the treatment of delinquents.

In 1960 Dr. Charles W. Slack published a paper on "Experimenter-Subject Psychotherapy," describing the work he had started at Harvard in January 1958. At that time his research dealt primarily with conscientious objectors and he needed several delinquents with records of assault and battery as a control group. The purpose of the research was to determine differences between these two groups as measured by psychological tests. Dr. Slack called the director of a local settlement house and asked whether she knew of any boys with suitable court records who would like to earn several dollars a week by taking psychological tests. She referred several boys to the Center for Research in Personality on the Harvard campus where Dr. Slack had his office and laboratory. These boys, employed as experimental subjects, came to the laboratory several times a week to talk into a tape recorder about their dreams and fantasies. At the end of each hour they were paid in cash and asked to come at a set time for the next meeting. To his surprise Dr. Slack noticed that these boys, initially quite hostile toward psychological testing, developed an attachment to him, and that their previously irregular attendance at the laboratory soon became regular. Also, the social workers and parole officers concerned reported that the number of offenses committed by them apparently decreased.

At that time Dr. Slack and an associate were teaching a

seminar on research methods in psychotherapy. As a student in the seminar, I heard Dr. Slack describe his work with delinquents and conscientious objectors at an evening meeting. My imagination was immediately stirred both by the charismatic personality of Dr. Slack and by the possibility that seriously delinquent offenders—the leather-jacketed motorcycle crowd, for example—might be reached and powerfully affected by psychological techniques through the simple procedure of paying them for their cooperation. But could it be that this technique of paying delinquents as experimental subjects was a mere expediency? Or worse, perhaps it was only a clever deception that might eventually harm both the experimenter and the delinquents.

The informality of the seminar permitted me to ask Dr. Slack these and other questions. Our discussion lasted late that evening and continued on an almost daily basis for the next several weeks. Meanwhile, I observed several interview sessions and decided that I would also like to employ several delinquents as experimental subjects to talk into a tape recorder. Their job, however, should be slightly different. Instead of talking primarily about their dreams and fantasies, they should be permitted to talk about whatever they wanted (but preferably about themselves) with a minimum of verbal direction from the experimenter. If a boy should be unable to think of something to talk about, he would be reminded that it was his job to think of topics to talk about and any topic would be all right. If the boy still should be unable to think of a topic and should become anxious, the experimenter might suggest a topic that would very gradually guide the boy to discuss his own thoughts and feelings. For this the boy would be paid one to two dollars an hour. The objective was to design a therapeutic job which would be so "incredibly" simple that the delinquents could not fail to respond and succeed in it.

During the several weeks in which I observed Dr. Slack two new problems emerged. The first was that the delinquents employed by Dr. Slack began to spend much of their time during the day lounging around the laboratory or wandering through the building. They could occasionally be found making themselves a sandwich in the staff's small kitchen or sitting in the most comfortable leather chairs in the library with their feet propped up on the table. In general, their behavior was tolerated and accepted because they were viewed as somewhat "sick" individuals; certainly they were not considered to be a very "wholesome" group or one that could contribute greatly to scholastic endeavor. However, oblivious to their social standing among staff and students—or regardless of it—the delinquents began to invite their friends to the laboratory to wait for them while they talked into the tape recorder. These friends generally gathered in a small room, on the second floor of the building next to Dr. Slack's office, where they listened to music (usually rock-and-roll or Sinatra-type sounds) and played cards. Frequently, the sound of music and card playing would drift through the building down to the main business office on the first floor.

The second problem that developed at this time was in the area of public relations. Several social workers who previously had been enthusiastic about the research became increasingly skeptical. As rumors about the project spread through the delinquent subculture of Cambridge, several delinquents insisted, with characteristic bravado, that their social workers should pay them for interviews. A typical comment to a social worker was: "I can earn more at Harvard, why should I talk to you?" Although this situation was eventually resolved, when the delinquents realized that Harvard was not going to hire all of them, it did not in the meantime promote good will.

These two problems, the skeptical view of the research

by some social workers and the disturbance caused by the delinquents at the Center, were important factors in determining the future direction of the research project. To avoid further disturbance at the Center, another place was needed in which to interview the delinquents whom I wanted to employ. Through the efforts of my twin brother, who was also a student at Harvard, a laboratory was set up in a large storefront on a street corner in a respectable business district in Cambridge. This storefront, which previously had been a foreign-car showroom, was donated by a local business organization. The first few boys employed by me at this location helped to construct the laboratory facilities and suggested the name. For them it was obvious. The project was located on a street corner and did research. Hence, "Streetcorner Research." I do not believe that any of them had ever read *Street-corner Society* by W. F. Whyte.

Without the close cooperation of the social workers, it became difficult to employ delinquents through the previous procedure of referral from a social worker. Furthermore, we became increasingly interested in the very serious offenders who refused to cooperate with standard social agency programs. Since these "unreachable" delinquents did not, by definition, cooperate with established programs, it was necessary to meet them on the street corner, in the pool room, or wherever they spent their time.

After two to three weeks of hesitation, it became clear that I was going to have to frequent such places, or be unable to contact the delinquents whom I wanted to employ. On St. Patrick's Day, an enthusiastically celebrated holiday in Boston among many working-class people, a friend and I drove to the Washington Street area in downtown Boston at about ten P.M. The Washington Street locale is a well-known entertainment area with a relatively high crime rate. We were dressed in the typical collegiate style of chino slacks, white shirt, sweater, and loafers. My strategy was to be as honest as possible and to offer directly the job of experimental subject to the delinquent. This decision to be direct and honest came not so much from an overabundance of virtue as from an inability to tell convincing lies or to think of other alternatives. After walking around the area for approximately forty-five minutes, we spotted a likely looking prospect and his buddy standing in a doorway next to a bar. He was wearing the characteristic "uniform" of delinquents at that time, black chinos, leather jacket, and duck-tail haircut. While my friend watched from across the street, I walked up to him, immediately introduced myself as a student who needed someone to help me out in my research on delinquency, and offered him the job of talking into a tape recorder at one to two dollars an hour, if he had a court record. I mentioned that his friend could also come along and earn a dollar or two. He replied that he had been in reform school and that he needed some money right away so that he could buy some vodka to celebrate St. Patrick's Day. I assured him that he would earn enough to buy some vodka and that he could do whatever he wanted with the money he earned. This was a regular job and what he did with the money was his business. He replied, "Can I bring along anything I have with me?" When I answered, "Yes," he wiggled his right hand so that a fairly large hammer slid out from the sleeve of his leather jacket into his palm. While I was standing there properly impressed, he commented that he would have to buy the vodka right away because the package stores would be closed by the time he was finished talking into the recorder. In my enthusiasm not to lose this excellent prospective subject, I replied that I couldn't pay them ahead of time but that my friend had a half pint of vodka in the back of the car. They then agreed that they would come along to the laboratory to look over the job and we walked to the car. The fellow in the leather jacket got into the car first in the front seat. The bottle of vodka was lying on the back seat. He immediately reached around and flipped up the latch on the rear door. His buddy opened the door, grabbed the bottle, and both boys ran off through the alleys—their laughter echoing between the tall buildings. I was tricked, but more important than that, I had failed to employ a boy who was clearly on his way to trouble. And, as though this was not unfortunate enough, I had probably inadvertently contributed to this boy's delinquency by allowing him to get the vodka. I imagined the boy and his buddy getting drunk on some doorstep, laughing over their success, and going on to try their luck in breaking and entering or stealing a car.[1] With much sadness and disappointment my friend and I walked a few blocks to an amusement center. There we met Bill, the boy who became the first employee of Streetcorner Research. This meeting is described in detail in the following section on "Methods for Gaining Cooperation."

As the project expanded, we conducted an informal survey among our delinquent employees to determine the least likely places to which they would naturally go. These turned out to be a church and a police station. Subsequently, to test the effectiveness of our methods, we set up laboratories in a church and a city hall. (We were unable to find a police station that we could use.) The city hall had the additional advantage of being located in Lynn, Massachusetts, a medium-sized industrial city approximately forty minutes away from Boston by car. Because the delinquents in Lynn had not heard of Streetcorner

[1] Some two years later, while I was running group-therapy sessions in a medium-sized, medium-security prison in Massachusetts, one of the group members, after several weeks of participation, introduced himself as the boy who had made off with the vodka. He had been incarcerated for breaking and entering and the attempted blackmail of a physician.

Research, it was possible for us to retest the effectiveness of our procedures without either the positive or negative effects of a previously established reputation.

The project has been essentially a low-cost, low-overhead operation with no extensive investment in real estate or research equipment. The average cost per boy employed by the project for a nine-month period has been slightly under $400. This is considerably less than the usual cost of professional treatment for delinquents over a similar period of time, and much less than the cost of incarcerating a boy for nine months in Massachusetts (approximately $2200). The project has been financed primarily by personal donations from interested citizens and the experimenters. During difficult financial times contributions from private foundations and the Harvard Department of Social Relations made the continuation of the project possible.

The subjects who participated in our research were twenty-five delinquents and five non-delinquent boys from Cambridge, Boston, and Lynn; they were between the ages of fifteen and twenty-one. Of these boys, twenty were serious offenders with extensive court records who had spent at least six months or more in reform school or prison. Only four of these boys had held a job longer than six months and only one had completed high school. Eleven of these boys had actively refused to participate in such other delinquency-reduction programs in the community as individual therapy at a court clinic or settlement-house activities. Furthermore, they were all well-known to social workers and probation officers as "trouble makers" in the community. The majority of them came from families that were receiving state welfare payments. A few were from middle-class families. Nine were of Irish parentage, six Italian, ten English, and six undetermined by this study. Fourteen stated their religious preference as Catholic, eight as Protestant, and eight no preference. The majority were gang members. (For a more detailed description of the characteristics of the thirty boys see Appendix A.)

These boys were employed as experimental subjects or research assistants in various experimental activities to help the experimenters find new methods for reducing adolescent crime. They worked at the laboratory approximately one hour a day from two to five days a week for a period of nine to twelve months. They were paid immediately in cash each day following their work. The wages for these boys ranged from fifty cents to two dollars an hour. Data regarding their activities and their views of the world and themselves was continually collected and recorded. In addition, the experimenters eagerly sought the boys' own suggestions as to how their delinquent activities might be reduced. In a sense then, the boys were not only experimental subjects but also coworkers with the experimenters in finding new ways to change their behavior (Slack and Schwitzgebel, 1960; Schwitzgebel, 1960).

These boys participated in a wide variety of experimental activities. The directors of the project carefully selected these activities to provide both psychological data and a therapeutic potential for reducing crime. For example, the major research emphasis of the project was on the tape-recorded interviews. These interviews provided much valuable data about the delinquents and about delinquency in the Cambridge-Boston area. At the same time, these interviews helped several boys gain valuable insight into their own criminal activity. As a result of this insight, these boys committed significantly fewer crimes. This reduction in crime was considered a by-product of the boys' participation in the research activities. (A statistical analysis of the results of the Streetcorner Research project may be found in Appendix C.)

The experimental activities used in addition to the tape-recorded interviews were designated by the project as "secondary" activities. These activities included, among others, building electronic equipment, card playing, group discussions, and rewriting a driver's handbook.

Essentially, the Streetcorner Research project evolved out of the mutual experiences of the experimenters and the delinquents working toward certain specific objectives. Thus, it developed gradually; it did not begin with a logical design later given to others to complete. While this allowed for a very flexible response to the problems of working with the delinquent subculture, it also created its own problems, such as the frequent need to modify our financial plans and to develop techniques initially not well understood by the community.

Gaining the cooperation of the boys whom we wanted to have participate in our program was viewed as a three-step process. These three steps were first, to make a positive initial contact; second, to establish reliable attendance at the laboratory, and third, to obtain active participation in the laboratory activities. This three-step process developed during the first few months of our success and failure in gaining cooperation. Gradually, we came to realize that many non-working delinquents had forgotten or had never learned how to schedule their time. Their failure to attend the scheduled meetings of the project was more likely a result of their inability to follow a plan of activities rather than of a lack of interest or of hostility. Therefore, one of our first objectives was to "teach" them how to cooperate.

1. Making a Positive Initial Contact

The initial contact with a prospective subject was made by an experimenter calling a boy on the phone or meeting him on the street corner. He was offered a job as an experimental subject, and told that most of the fellows liked it. If the boy seemed reluctant, the name of a respected gang member who already had this job would be mentioned. The experimenter attempted to answer any details which the boy wanted to know directly and honestly. Finally, the boy was encouraged to bring a friend along, just to look over the job, and then to make up his mind.

The excerpt below may help to describe the nature of this initial contact. It is taken from a conversation which occurred in an amusement center between an experimenter and a prospective subject, whom we shall call Bill, on March 11, 1958. Bill and his friends gathered around a pinball machine on which I had just won nine free games. After I had given Bill several free games, the following conversation was recorded as nearly as possible by a friend who had come along for this purpose. I had not met Bill previously.[2]

EXPERIMENTER: Have you ever been in trouble with the cops?

BILL: No, not me. How come you ask? [Bill is caught off guard by the direct question. He thinks perhaps this guy is a cop.]

EXPERIMENTER: Well, that's too bad because if you'd been in some trouble I might have a job for you. [Bill is really surprised now. Maybe this guy is some new kind of cop. Or maybe he's a queer. Anyway, things are getting interesting.]

BILL: What do you mean? Do you want me to roll drunks or what?

EXPERIMENTER: No, it's a different kind of job. We're trying to find out how come kids get into trouble and what to do about it. So the only way to find out is to ask them. You just talk into a tape recorder about anything you want, but mostly about yourself. You can get up to two dollars an hour. You don't get rich 'cause you only work a couple of hours a week, but it's good pocket money. We want to find out why kids get into trouble so we ask them and they tell us.

BILL: You're not a cop, are you? [Bill doesn't really believe the experimenter. Who ever heard of a "straight" job that required a police record?]

EXPERIMENTER: No, we don't want to know names or places or anything like that. Just what's happened to you, and what you think about things. I'd like some coffee; let's talk about it over here. [Both walk over to the lunch counter on the other side of the amusement center and order coffee. Experimenter

---

[2] This friend, acting as an observer, took notes during the conversation. The following, therefore, is not verbatim, but is reconstructed from notes and memory as accurately as possible.

pays for both.] It's a job. We're doing research. It's an experiment, and you get paid for being one of the guys in it. I know it sounds corny. We've got a little white rat at the lab and we're teaching him to do tricks. That's his part in the experiment. Other people do other things. Your job would be talking into a recorder.

BILL: You mean I'm a guinea pig? [He is beginning to get the idea of the job. He is also a little pleased that someone is seeking him out for a legitimate job.]

EXPERIMENTER: That's right. Some of the guys call it guinea-pigging. Most all of them like it, and bring their friends around for a job; but we like to start with new guys who don't know us.

BILL: Say, you're not a bug doctor, are you? [Fear of the psychiatrist is intense. To associate with one voluntarily in gang territory would immediately cause the loss of gang prestige and protection.]

EXPERIMENTER: No, I just help out. I'm a student. There's other people like me, and there's Dr. Slack. He's the big man who runs the outfit. He's a prof. at the school where we run the experiment.

BILL: You're not a bug doctor, huh? If you are, I won't go.

EXPERIMENTER: No, I just help out with the experiment. You get paid in cash, and you can quit whenever you want to. You've really got to see the place before you make up your mind. It's a pretty good deal, and it's on the level. But maybe you don't have a bad enough record, because we need kids who've done time. You look like you've been around.

BILL: I've done time.

EXPERIMENTER: Good. Let's take a look at the place. You can bring your friend along. Look it over, then make up your mind. Nothing to lose, and it's something to do.

Bill nodded yes and talked briefly with a friend. Then we all took the subway to the Harvard campus. While at the lab, they ate an enormous number of cookies, drank several cokes, whistled into the tape recorder, and talked about how bad reform school is. They used false names. At the end of the hour, Bill was paid two dollars. On the way back to the amusement center, the boys asked me when the *real* job started—meaning when do we roll the drunks or do the actual work. The purpose of the project was explained again. The next day we met at the same place at the same time and went to the lab. After several meetings, the boy commented, "You mean I get paid for just talking?"

This fairly typical series of events suggests some of the problems involved in meeting a prospective subject for the first time. Naturally, Bill was suspicious. Why was a stranger being nice to him? He figured that behind the kindness there was some hidden motive which would eventually be to his disadvantage. The experimenter was nearly always seen in the role of a homosexual, cop, big-time operator in the underworld, or a psychiatrist looking for interesting cases.

The most frequent and immediate perception of the experimenter was that of a homosexual. This was not entirely unrealistic since delinquent and homosexual populations are often involved in activities of mutual exploitation. However, this perception was weakened when the experimenter asked Bill to bring a friend along and mentioned the name of a gang leader who already had the job. Nor did the experimenter fit into the role of a cop, since he did not want to know names or places and did not make an arrest. He did not act like a big-time operator because he did not flash a lot of money or suggest an illegal job. And, finally, he did not appear to be a "bug doctor" because he paid money, ran experiments, and did not work in a hospital or clinic. In the same way the most convincing artifacts in the laboratory turned out to be the electronic equipment and the white rat. These made the experimental activities appear "scientific" rather than "therapeutic." The rat was originally purchased for use in a research project, but the desire of the boys to torture it did not make this feasible.

2. Establishing Reliable Attendance at the Laboratory

Whether the boy came to the laboratory by himself or was met on the street first by the experimenter, his arrival at the laboratory was immediately rewarded or reinforced with soft drinks, fruit, or sandwiches. At the end of the hour, the boy was paid in cash for his work. If the boy came to the laboratory by himself, a meeting was generally set for the next day at the same time at the laboratory. If the boy was met on the street, the next meeting was generally set for the next day at the same time and at the same place on the street.

An attempt was made to create a nurturant atmosphere in the laboratory. Care was taken, however, not to make a display of wealth or to offer more than could be accepted easily. For these reasons, particular use was made of the *sharing* of food by experimenter and subject. To share a single item such as an orange was found much more effective than to give several to a boy if an experimenter did not eat any. In a few cases, the boys would not accept food, even when quite hungry, unless the experimenter began eating first.

Most of the difficulty in obtaining attendance at the laboratory was with those boys who had to be met initially on the street. If a boy did not arrive for his second meeting within several hours of the proper time, an experimenter would look for him again at the places where he usually spent his time. If he was found, he and the experimenter would go back to the laboratory. If he was not found, the experimenter would return to the place where he had met the boy initially and wait for him the next day. The boys generally arrived dependably at the laboratory by themselves within two to seven meetings.

In six difficult cases, we used a procedure somewhat similar to that used for the "shaping" of animal behavior in a psychological laboratory. In these cases, the boys were met at successively closer geographical locations to the laboratory. For example, the first two meetings with Bill and Henry were at an amusement center in downtown Boston. The next meeting was outside a subway station near the amusement center, then inside the subway station *before* the toll gate, then inside the subway station *after* the toll gate, then outside the subway station at Harvard Square, and then finally at the laboratory. On each of these occasions when a boy arrived at the proper place—however early or late—his arrival was immediately rewarded by the experimenter. Most often the reward was a cigarette or part of a candy bar. Sometimes it was money (when an experimenter put a token in the toll gate for a boy) or the announcement of something particularly interesting planned for the day. Also, of course, the mere presence of an experimenter was often rewarding for a boy. Rewards were given as immediately and naturally as possible. An experimenter, for example, would pull out a cigarette for himself when a boy arrived and then offer him one. A boy's natural response was to take one if he wanted it. (There was no "charity" involved here that might hurt a boy's pride since it is customary to offer a friend a cigarette while having one yourself.) The shaping of attendance took approximately two weeks in each case.

Finally, the *attitude* of the experimenters toward the attendance problem must be mentioned. The problem of delinquent nonattendance was considered to be very different from the problem of nonattendance at therapy sessions by middle-class neurotic patients. If a middle-class person pays for therapy and then fails to attend, it may be a sign of the severity of his problem. He has had much experience with keeping appointments and recognizes their importance. If a delinquent fails to attend a meeting, he may be merely out swimming and will show up the next day without realizing the inconvenience he has caused. In the Boston working-class delinquent subculture there are two primary modes of meeting—by habit (delinquents almost always appear at a particular corner at a particular time) and by impulse ("I'll see you around"). Even in the matter of dating, which is quite important, these boys will rarely call a girl in advance. The usual procedure is to find a car first and then to drive to the girl's home—getting angry, of course, if she is not there.

We had no legal or political power to force or coerce prospective subjects into attending. They could only be invited, encouraged, and rewarded for their attendance. If a boy failed to attend, we interpreted this to mean that the laboratory situation was not attractive enough for him, or he had forgotten about the meeting, or it might have been because he had not yet learned to keep appointments. Most of the boys missed several meetings before their attendance became dependable. The solution to this was to increase the incentives for attendance, to set a time for another meeting, and to let each boy know that no matter how many meetings he missed he was still welcome. From our viewpoint, as long as the prospective subject could be found and talked with, employment was still a possibility. In one particularly recalcitrant case, an experimenter and a project assistant, an attractive blond girl, drove to the boy's home, in a low-rent housing project, in a Thunderbird convertible. The boy and his friends were immediately impressed and eagerly came along to the laboratory just for the ride. Afterwards the boy commented, "It was just like out of the movies when you drove up."

Under these conditions, attendance became dependable (that is, the boy would arrive at the laboratory sometime during the day of his appointment) with all but two of the boys contacted by this study. In these two cases one boy was arrested and sent to reform school after his first meeting, and the other boy, after the first two interviews, obtained another job that took up most of his available hours.

Even after the boys could be expected to arrive at the laboratory dependably for their meetings, they were still sometimes as much as three hours early or late. The purpose of the second stage was to shape their behavior into arriving on time. This was attempted *only* after the experimenter was sure that a given boy would arrive sometime during the day for his meeting. The more nearly a boy's time of arrival corresponded to his appointment time, the more likely he was able to work for the full hour and obtain full pay. Boys were paid only for the work they completed. If, for example, a boy arrived one hour late, he might be allowed to work only forty-five minutes instead of his usual hour. Thus, it was to his financial advantage to arrive on time.

Also, subjects were occasionally given bonuses when they arrived on time. Most often these bonuses were money (twenty-five to fifty cents), but sometimes they were gifts, for example, tickets to a baseball game. The bonus was given immediately upon the boy's arrival, and it was explained to him that it was for his prompt arrival. In general, the conditions suggested by Eissler (1950) for gift-giving to delinquents were followed, that is, the experimenters attempted to give bonuses when they were not expected and when they would not hurt the boy's pride or make him feel obligated.

Initially, the time for meetings was set at the boy's convenience. This meant that most of the meetings were held in the late afternoon or early evening. For some subjects the first several meetings were held at night or early in the morning after the bars closed (1 A.M.). Gradually a time was set that was somewhat more convenient for the experimenter. Typically, the boy's initial attendance at the laboratory fluctuated widely—from several hours early to several hours late—and during the first few weeks he might completely miss three or four meetings. Then, attendance would gradually become more dependable until, at the end of thirteen to twenty meetings, the boy would arrive regularly and on time.

3. Obtaining Active Participation in the Laboratory Activities

The final step in gaining attendance and cooperation was getting the boys to come to the laboratory to participate in its activities. To encourage this cooperation the experimenters attempted to create a laboratory "subculture" in which the rules, values, and objectives of the laboratory were transmitted from the older boys to the younger boys in much the same way that a street gang perpetuates its own culture. When a boy arrived at the laboratory, he was told as few rules as necessary. No list of regulations or objectives were given to him. When he asked about the operation of the laboratory, the answer given to him was something like this (from mimeographed instructions for experimenters):

We are interested in studying and understanding teenagers, especially those who have been in trouble. We are not trying to "straighten out" anybody. If you want to straighten out, you will have to do that on your own. When you work here in the experiments and take tests and talk into the tape recorder, you are helping us to understand the feelings, attitudes, and actions of teenagers. We want to know why kids foul up and why they do the other things they do. We figure you may help us find some of the answers.

We have two rules around here: first, nobody has to do anything if he really doesn't want to do it. Second, nobody gets paid for anything he doesn't do. In general, if you want to know anything, ask one of the older guys who has been around longer. We do try to help the boys and you probably know some of the guys we helped to get jobs and in other ways. We don't *have* to help anybody though. And nobody needs to take the help who doesn't want it.

If you have any complaints, take them right to the manager. If you have any idea about what's wrong or how we aren't doing the right thing here, tell us. That's one of the things we are paying you for—to tell us what our mistakes are so we can do better next time. We listen to you and record what you say; you are *our* teachers. If you learn too, that's O.K., but we are not in the business to teach you. We are not responsible for you. Nobody referred you to us; you weren't sent here by the court or any other agency. We picked you out because you were a kid in trouble or looked up to by the other guys or knew about reform school and other kinds of things and feelings we want to study. You don't have to work for us and we don't have to hire you.

Everybody is free around here. If you destroy the place, you lose a good deal and we lose our data; nobody benefits. The worst thing we can do is fire you, then you won't get what we have to offer and we lose a good subject. [Actually, no boys were ever fired, but one was suspended temporarily for stealing twenty dollars from an experimenter's coat pocket.] We don't want to lose our subjects. We need them because without them we would not be in business. However, there are lots of subjects we could use out on the streets so nobody should get a swelled head. When you foul up in your life you don't hurt us because we can't be blamed for it. But we are human too, we really like our subjects and we hate to see them get hurt and get in trouble. For this reason we want to help them stay out of trouble if they want to. Once you are in trouble, it is a mess and there is very little we can do for you. When you are on probation, you can't get a driver's license, it is very hard for you to get good jobs, the Army won't take you, and the courts run your life and you have to take it from them and like it. We can do one hundred percent more for guys who are not in trouble. We can help them get jobs and licenses, take them on trips and so on. But we can't get you out of trouble once you are in it. We have very little pull. We never pay bondsmen—it's just one of the rules. If you get sent away, all we can do is come visit you. We really only study trouble; we can't beat it once it gets started.

The general policy was one of "openness" about the activities of the project. Most of the boys were curious and were encouraged by the experimenters to ask the other boys questions or to read publications or correspondence related to the project. The experimenters and boys agreed that they could ask each other any question they wanted, but there were two conditions: 1) the person asked did not have to answer the question if he did not want to answer, and 2) all questions were to be answered honestly. In other words, inquiry was encouraged but the right to privacy was made explicit, and maintained. In general, the experimenters tended to answer cautiously questions regarding the state and source of funds for the project, biographical data about individual subjects, and their personal lives. The many other areas of interest related to the project were open for almost unlimited inquiry. The boys seemed to appreciate very much the opportunity to ask questions and to know at the same time that inappropriate questions would not make the experimenter angry.

1. Tape-Recorded Interviews

The types of interviewing done with the subjects ranged from philosophical discussion through moral guidance to psychoanalytic on-the-couch interviewing. Nearly all of the interviewing began by allowing the boy to talk randomly about whatever he wanted and then gradually shifted to the particular style of the experimenter. These interviews were held three to five times a week for an hour at a time.

The various types of interviews clearly reflected the different professional backgrounds of the experimenters. The graduate student in education attempted interviewing from a philosophical viewpoint. The psychologist, whose training included psychoanalysis, conducted the psychoanalytically oriented interviews. The social worker and the graduate student in social work used a psychiatric casework approach. The Jesuit priest conducted interviews that were religiously oriented.

The interviewing by the student in education. The interviewing done by the graduate student in education can best be described as "philosophical discussion." It was an attempt to combine philosophical content with psychological process.

Within this philosophical perspective, the delinquent was not viewed primarily as sick, disobedient, or the product of a delinquent subculture (although none of these possibilities were completely eliminated). The perspective was rather that certain cases of delinquency result primarily from a philosophical position which is in conflict with the legally sanctioned structures of society. For these particular "philosophical offenders," crime is not essentially a leisure-time activity or a profession to gain money or power. It is more nearly a revolt aimed at the destruction of certain customs of sociey. Its emotional force is derived from a profound discontent that is combined with anger and a search for thrills.

At the intellectual level, the philosophy of this revolt is a curious and unsystematic combination of ideas from Sartre, Genet, Nietzsche, De Sade, Heidegger, and others. These ideas, frequently taken out of context, contain two central themes: 1) social protest based upon a repudiation of man's progress, and 2) secular existentialism. The outlook is destructive without the obligation of being constructive. There is primarily only the moment to be lived with as much courage as possible. One of the early documents presenting this view was the "Futurist Manifesto" issued in 1919 in Italy. A few lines may suggest its general tone:

> The furious sweep of folly snatched us from ourselves and chased us over the ways, precipitous and deep as the beds of torrents, and we, like young lions, were bent on pursuing death. Let us give ourselves to the unknown, though not through desperation, but only to brim up the deep wells of the absurd. We will extol aggressive, feverish insomnia, the double-quick step, the somersault, the box on the ear, fisticuffs. We declare that the splendor of the world has been enriched by a new beauty: the beauty of speed . . . Burn the libraries, break the courses of the canals in order to inundate the museums; demolish, demolish the venerated cities![3]

After skimming off the rhetorical foam of this statement, Kahler (1957, p. 147) suggests that we can easily recognize here "the traces of Nietzsche's barbarism, of Baudelairian satanism and egotism. But the question of values, even of

[3] As quoted in Erich Kahler, *The Tower and the Abyss* (New York: Braziller, 1957), pp. 146–147.

a transvaluation of values, is not raised any longer. It is the eruption of superforces, a Storm and Stress, such as had stirred the youth of many periods before. Its new feature, however, is its aimlessness." Here, perhaps, is the beginning of the present-day, youthful preoccupation with technology, not because it is useful but because of its intense stimulating effects through speed and power. The contemporary image is of a group of motorcyclists intently weaving and roaring their way through dense city traffic without any particular destination; their purpose is only to be suspended by immediate sensation between speed and power on one side and dramatic accident and pain on the other.

The subjects interviewed on the basis of this philosophical perspective typically moved through a sequence of clearly noticeable stages that may be characterized as apathy, anger, despair, insight, and philosophical transformation (Schwitzgebel, 1960; Schwitzgebel, 1963a). These stages will be described in part, by using excerpts from interviews with eighteen-year-old Bill, who was in reform school for the first time at the age of twelve. A court psychologist and a probation officer described him in court records as "unreachable," and a psychiatrist employed by his family diagnosed him as "psychopathic with atypical EEG patterns." His IQ was within the normal range at 108. At the time of his employment by the project, he had been out of reform school for two months and had recently run away from home. His police record included breaking and entering, drunkenness, rape, assault, illegal possession of firearms, suspicion of auto theft, and larceny.

A detailed study of this boy is particularly useful in illustrating the change that occurs through the interviewing technique. Bill was unusually skillful in expressing his feelings and even to the last interview retained his native mode of expression. Instead of using the psychiatric term, "repression," he said, "something grinding away in my heart like it is trying to break the doors down." And instead of using the term, "depression," he said, "downhearted." His feelings, as he describes them, validate analytic theory and, yet, are not produced as an artifact of learning psychiatric language. Also, since Bill was the first boy interviewed in the Streetcorner Research situation, the sequence of stages through which he went could not have resulted from prior knowledge or expectation.

Apathy. Throughout the interview sessions Bill was allowed to talk about whatever he wanted. During his first hour at the laboratory he decided that he would like to be employed by the project and so, to demonstrate his qualifications for the job, he talked about his experience in reform school. The following are his first recorded words:[4]

BILL: Well, when you first enter training school you go to the big office. Then you meet the superintendent. He shoots you a lot of bull. Tells you what to do and what not to do. Then he sends for a boy and he takes you down to get a haircut. They cut all your hair off. Then they issue you clothes, they give you all the clothes and shoes you'll need. They then take you to a big cottage. In the cottage, you get there about 12 o'clock, maybe you eat dinner before you go to the cottage. Then you go to the cottage. [Laughs uneasily at his buddy.] So you sit around there, maybe rest of the day. Go to the receiving cottage first. You stay in the receiving cottage two weeks, working on the farm. Hard work. Then after your two weeks is up, you get a trade, maybe. You go to school half a day and you work a half a day, and get half a day Saturday off, get Sunday off. And they have-ah, most of them have print shops, laundry, big dining room, farm, cannery, gym, school—

---

4 The excerpts from the tape-recorded interviews presented in this book have been transcribed as accurately as possible by research assistants. Names, places, and other identifying information as well as certain hesitancies and redundancies have been edited out.

the work I did was printing. You learn a lot 'cause they make you learn a lot. You know you learn a lot. If you don't do what they tell you to then they give it to you right—you know what I mean, right. They whip you, they whip you hard.

EXPERIMENTER: They do?

BILL: Yea. This other boy I was rooming with, he was a real brain, you know. Cause I was pretty smart but he was a brain. He could make keys to fit coke machines, paper machines, we'd just clean up on it, we had it knocked, break into parking meters, things like that . . .

During the first few interviews, Bill would usually talk about how bad prison was, how the cops were always after him for nothing, how fate was against him, and so on. He talked primarily to earn money. Gradually, however, he ran out of things to say. He was then told that thinking of topics to talk about was a part of his job. The experimenter only occasionally suggested a topic. When a topic was suggested it was usually related to something personally important to the boy so that the talking gradually shifted toward the boy's talking about himself. It was clearly understood, however, that the boy was always free to reject the experimenter's suggestion and talk about whatever he wished.

Anger. As Bill realized that he could talk without being criticized, his language became increasingly hostile. This anger was directed toward the law, the family, social customs, the experimenter, or randomly toward people who were irritating. His expression of anger became most frequent between the third and eleventh interviews.

For example, as Bill entered the laboratory for his fourth interview, he observed that the experimenter's tie was the "crummiest" he had ever seen. Later, during the hour while Bill was talking into the recorder, a construction worker outside the laboratory yelled some instructions to his partner. Bill pointed toward the window and commented, "See

that guy out there? Going to mash his mouth in." Toward
the end of the hour, he described an incident from back
home:

I cut him from his navel around to his back. He was down
on his knees yelling, "Help me, help me." I turned around and
I just had to laugh—I don't know why. The next morning I read
about it in the paper. I don't know why, but whenever I see
something like that I have to laugh. Like if someone would fall
out of that window, or whenever I see a wreck it's funny.

During the same hour he made the following comment
about cops:

Cops, there ain't no damn telling what they are. Crooks are
good people. Yeah, I wish that god damned guy'd shut up.
Going to go out there and mash his mouth in a minute. [Pause
—some noise made outside by construction workers.] What
the hell's that? If I could do it I swear I'd get rid of every cop
there is. I'd just get rid of them. Boy, I'd mow 'em down
bigger'n shit. I would, I'd find a way to get rid of them. The
bad ones that is. All of them ain't a son of a bitch, but most
of 'em are.

During the next hour of interviewing, Bill presented his
view of a visit to a psychiatrist:

That son of a bitch, I was getting ready to turn around and
knock the hell out of him. He comes in there and he says, "Take
off your god damned clothes." I say, "What for?" and he said,
"Take off your goddam clothes." I take off my clothes. The old
nurse comes in there. Get the god damn hell out of here will
ya? He lays me down on that table and he starts poking around
with a hammer [to test reflexes]. Get that god damn hammer
away from me. He tells me turn over. And I turn over, and he
jams his finger right up my ass. God damn I jumped for a
country mile. Son of a bitch run in the next room and brought
me in there and talked to me and asked me a bunch of questions. Said, "Is there anything you want to tell me?" I said,
"Hell, no, I don't want to tell you a god damned thing." He
went out there and told my old lady I was crazy and I was

going to go back there and beat the hell out of him. Wouldn't let me. That guy was luny. Crazy as a bat! The way all those guys around here [Harvard] are, and that's where he came from too, one of these places.

EXPERIMENTER: Then you didn't, uh, you didn't like him telling you you were crazy.

BILL: Heck, no, I didn't like it.

EXPERIMENTER: How come then, how come you didn't like him saying you're crazy?

BILL: Crazy. If he was giving me some money I'd talk some different turkey. I knew the same thing he told me, as far as I wasn't crazy, I know that. He just getting the money, that's what he was getting, that's what all of them got, except me, I got a year in the god damn reform school. God damnedest place I ever been in.

EXPERIMENTER: How much money?

BILL: $400. That's for sticking them damn pins [EEG electrodes] in my head, you know. Laid there on his old fucking couch, I know what I laid on—stick a few pins in her [the nurse].

During this period of anger, the experimenter was somewhat more active than during the previous period of apathy. He would ask the subject to explain his angry feelings in more detail or inquire what it was about a particular situation that made the boy angry. The purpose of obtaining these details was not to intensify the anger for catharsis. Rather, it was hoped that as the goals or wishes being blocked became more specifically defined for the boy, the anger would become more controlled.

The period of anger lasted approximately three weeks for Bill. For other boys in the project this period of anger varied roughly from three to eight weeks. This time seemed to depend in part upon how frequently the boy was seen; however, the cases are too few to reach a conclusion in this regard. For Bill, the transition from anger to the next period of despair occurred over two or three weeks during which statements of a hostile or depressive tone alternated.

Despair. This period was the most difficult for both Bill and the experimenter. The characteristics were clear. The boy suffered. He experienced loneliness, depression, sorrow, and sometimes fear and guilt. Ultimately, this despair would become so deep that in Kierkegaard's terms it was a "sickness unto death." These words are meant literally. The following excerpts are taken from the sixteenth to twentieth hours:

. . . I'm scared. Whenever I get in a fight or anything I'm shaking like a leaf. Anything! I'm just plain scared—that's [unclear]. I wouldn't admit it to nobody but you, but I was scared awful. Last four years. Scared to walk the streets, scared to go out of my house, scared to stay there. And in a way I want to go to prison, just, just, it's there. I could do something there, something. Just work, if I'd get five [years], just work so I could get out in three—for the hell of it.

This ain't me sitting here, that's for damn sure, this ain't me for a long time ago. It's somebody that thrives from day to day. Don't ever give a damn. What worries me, "What the hell's going to happen to me?" [long pause] Where'd I mess up along the way? Trying to figure it out. Figure out the day that I started stealing. Can't figure out when that day'd be.

Maybe that's it. Maybe I'm scared of something. Maybe there's something way back there I'm scared of. Something that happened. [unclear] Or maybe I just, I just know something's going to happen to me, soon. Or when I started doing it [crime], it was going to happen to me in a period of years and I was trying to get everything in soon as I could. Could be too. But then again I got my doubts about that because I think, I think of what's going to happen to me. I think of what I'm going to be. And I know there's no hope left to be anything—important. You know, shit. Going to be a busboy all my life? [tearful] I never did look ahead. I looked to what was happening then. The only thing I looked ahead to was the bad things I was going to do. Something must have happened somewhere. I can't think of it. Maybe I seen my daddy murder somebody or something [embarrassed laugh].

And then we moved, we moved on ——— road and I remember going to school and these boys talked me into breaking in that house and I did. And I remember stealing in '52 and I went to jail and my daddy got me out without going to court and it cost him his '52 Ford. He had to sell it. That's where it started. Started stealing everything! [unclear] If I could just, just think of why I got that money, out of that boy's, that first bank. I remember, I remember real clear I took it in my pocket in the basement and I counted it and I looked at it; it was just a whole big bunch of it and I was real scared. I took it out and buried it. It was the first time. And I started taking money out of my mother's and daddy's pockets, when I got just a little older, a couple or three months. And I remember the day I got $10 out of my mother's pocketbook—and this boy went over and told on me and she didn't whip me, she never would. And we started breaking into houses and they went in [unclear] and I got a cigarette and some candies or something. And it just got in my blood. And the next, next day or week or something I just, I just went, boy.

Maybe that's it—maybe I'm scared of something. Maybe there's something way back there I'm scared of. Something that happened. Maybe I just . . . I just know something's going to happen to me [mumbles] . . . in a period of years, I was trying to get everything I could. I think of what's going to happen to me—of what I'm going to be. I know there's no hope left to be anything—important. You know shit, what am I going to be? a busboy all my life? Never did look ahead, looked to what was happening then. The only things I looked ahead to were the bad things I was going to do. Something must have happened somewhere [tearful, mumbles].

During this time the only food that Bill ate was that which the experimenter shared with him. This consisted largely of peanut butter—eaten directly out of the jar with a spoon—and coke or orange juice.

A new task now confronted the experimenter: he had to carefully watch for the health and safety of the boy. Rather than direct, deliberate attempts at self-harm, Bill displayed a profound carelessness about himself. Typical careless behavior by Bill and the other boys who went through this period of despair was smoking in bed, not eating, failure to complete routine obligations, etc. Legal violations usually resulted from a thoughtless lack of concern rather than from direct anger. Mild neurotic symptoms were noticed such as headaches, nausea, fear of ulcers, and nervous habits that frequently occur in the treatment of severe delinquents.

Typical questions asked by Bill during this period were, "What is going to happen to me?" or "Is there any hope left?" If the sorrow was deep enough, pretense was shattered. These questions became sincere, and the search for their answers honest. This honesty was considered critically important, for unless inquiry is honest, philosophical discussion is useless and becomes a game of wits. In the honest search, the person opens himself to the impact of his discoveries.

At this point the interviewing, or philosophical discussion, differed radically from traditional psychotherapy. In response to the boy's honest questions, the experimenter began gradually to explain his own experiences or the experiences of others. He presented his own values, beliefs, and doubts. This presentation was low-key, humble, unrushed, and as sincere as possible. Sometimes it involved embarrassment as well as enthusiasm, and was not intended to overwhelm the boy. Care was taken to explain to the boy that he was under no obligation to accept the ideas of the experimenter. He was free to reject them, change them, contradict them, or leave the experimental situation completely. Further, he should realize that the experimenter cannot really answer questions for him. Beliefs or opinions of the experimenter apply only to the experimenter himself. The experimenter refused to say, "you should," or "you should not," even to the question of crime. As Jung (1958, p. 66) has noted:

The psychic situation of the individual is so menaced nowadays by advertisement, propaganda and other more or less well-meant advice and suggestions that for once in his life the patient might be offered a relationship that does not repeat the nauseating "you should," "you must," and similar confessions of impotence. Against the onslaught from outside no less than against its repercussions in the psyche of the individual the doctor sees himself obliged to play the role of counsel for the defense.

Because no ready-made answers were provided, there was no escape for the boy by placing responsibility for a decision on the experimenter. Each honest question eventually turned the boy toward himself. Yet, this unhappy, broken self to which the boy had to turn for answers was the very self which initially caused his unhappiness. Thus, the boy was often led to new experiences of suffering and sometimes to discovery.

Insight. Theodor Reik, (1933, p. 334) has suggested that the source of psychoanalytic insight (derived from unconscious knowledge) lies within suffering. He comments, "I purposely use the word 'suffering.' Not misfortune, not mere calamity, nor yet disastrous or sad experience thus bears fruit . . . The hurts which we sustain teach us caution, but suffering, consciously experienced and mastered, teaches us wisdom." Of course, suffering does not necessarily produce insight; on the other hand, when the process described here was successful it seemed to be a necessary prerequisite.[5]

[5] Perhaps Martin Buber has pointed to this same process within a more religious context in his book, *Between Man and Man* (Boston: Beacon, 1957). In the chapter, "Education of Character," he notes: "It is an idle

After several days of severe depression, Bill reported the following incident from the previous night:

BILL: Well about 7:30 last night I went in, in the house, and laid down and took off my clothes, you know, and figure how long it was going to take me to get my clothes that, you know, I've been wanting so bad. So I laid down in the bed, you know, tried to go to sleep. And all of a sudden I woke up and boy my heart was, it was just beating, and I felt real good all over. Excitement was just busting out all over me. [EXPERIMENTER: How long did you sleep?] I didn't sleep any. I just laying there. And you know I thought, I thought it was because I could get the money so soon and everything. But it wasn't. And all of a sudden I thought of [imagined] Ronald [Bill's best friend] being dead. And I thought of the tape recorder playing and I was talking of his death. And, then I got sudden fear, that fell over me, you know. And more excitement. And then I thought of what I'd say as I was talking in this tape recorder. And I said, "He's dead. He's dead. What am I going to do? He was a part of me. A brother, mother and dad combined into one. Oh Lord, what will I do? What would have to happen?" And, and you, "For the good talk, here's an extra dollar." And I said, "Money, money, the hell with money! What will I do?" Said, "Will I go back to the streets, the corners, drinking, and stealing?" And then it hit me. And I got the, the title of that poem automatically in my head—and my pen just wrote automatically. I, it just like I, the words just coming just like that. And the title of it was, "The Death of Part of Me." I'm going to have to read this.[6]

---

undertaking to call out, to a mankind that has grown blind to eternity, 'Look! the eternal values!' One has to begin by pointing to that sphere where man himself, in the hours of utter solitude, occasionally becomes aware of the disease through sudden pain; by pointing to the relation of the individual to his own self. In order to enter into a personal relation with the absolute, it is first necessary to be a person again . . . The desire to do this is latent in the pain the individual suffers through his distorted relation to his own self . . . To keep the pain awake, to waken the desire —that is the first task of everyone who regrets the obscuring of eternity" (pp. 110–111).

[6] The poem is presented here as the boy wrote it.

"The Death of Part of Me"

I look back through the
years and what do I see,
Somewhere, somehow
I lost a part of me.
I think, oh how I think
of the life I have lived,
The life of the devil.
Will anyone ever forgive?
Can I do right is there
a chance, can I ever
be free and yet I think, what
happened to that part of
me? The kindness and
gentleness that I was
gifted with. Will
anyone ever give me
a lift?
What made me steal,
cheat and lie? Will I
carry this secret never
knowing when I die
I know, I know.
I lost a part of me.

Now that seems, it, it, now that's *my writing*, and I want my
name under it. I wrote that. I wrote it, and I mean, I want,
I wrote it. No doubt about it. Now that this, as I say further,
this is going to seem funny, like it's been made up—that's what
it's going to seem like to other people, but, but I know and
you know it's true. And then I read it over and boy I read it
crying. I swear to God I cried and I ran down stairs and tried
to call you and I couldn't get you for an hour and a half.
I walked back and then I cried again. Man, every time I read
or thought about it I just started crying—I don't know why.
When all of the excitement was almost gone I went out and
bought this twenty-five cent tablet and wrote all of it down.

And, boy, I was real anxious, I was just so anxious and I thought am I coming close, and I went back to bed and it was raining and I felt aware, you know, of a new adventure like [unclear] it.

Experiences of this sudden intensity occurred in only two cases of which Bill was one. Generally, for the other boys, insight was more similar to a growth process made up of lesser, but deepening, discoveries over a period of several weeks or months. In two cases insight was not noticed or reported.

In each case where insight occurred, the content of the insight differed. For one subject, it was the realization that by continually fighting the law his life was actually being controlled by it. For another, it was understanding that morality and social customs are not always the same. For another, it was learning that insanity is not inherited. These discoveries do not seem very profound intellectually, but their power resides in their personal relevance and their synthesis with new emotional experiences.

Philosophical Transformation. A transformation did not occur immediately with psychological insight. Insight was only the beginning. After insight there were still the harmful influences of the boy's world and the realistic demands of society. At the very least, the boy had to conform to the routines of a job. The old emotions of apathy, anger, and despair, although less frequent, would still occur. Approximately two weeks after Bill expressed the insight quoted above he came in one Saturday morning drunk.

And I kicked her out in the morning, huh, made her walk home. I ain't got no heart. Hm, hm! And I got up this morning at eight o'clock and I had four bottles of beer left and I drank that and I sent the guy after a half a case and I drank that. And I got eight cans left and more money and I'm going right back and I'm going to drink again. Ha, ha, what do you think about that? [EXPERIMENTER: I think you're going to drink a

lot.] You're damned right I am. And tomorrow morning I'm going
to have the biggest headache and I'm going to feel the terriblest
and the horriblest that I ever felt in my life. Ha, I don't care.
I don't care about anything. Nothing [unclear]. Who can save
me? Hungry, lonely, over the hill, I'll live ragged and be a bum
all my life.

When the boy felt these old emotions again, he usually
thought that the experiment had not worked, that he had
been just fooling himself, or that the insight was real but
its effects had worn off. Nevertheless, he could not unsee
the possibilities he had seen—in somewhat the same manner that a person who has found the hidden image in a
scrambled picture cannot look at that picture again without seeing the image or knowing that it is there. He could
not "unhave" the insight experience. During the thirty-
second hour Bill commented:

Well, I don't know. You know, I just, I was doing so good,
I was making progress. You don't know, I don't think you know
anyway—that the progress I made to me, to me, man, you don't
know how it used to be. Man, I, I was a slob, a slut, a damned
hoodlum, boy, all the time. I don't mean just an hour a day
or two hours or twelve hours—twenty-four hours a day. I'd get
so sleepy that I'd have to go home and sleep for three or four
hours, then I'd head right back to town and start all over again.
I did everything. There wasn't a person I didn't know, a thing I
didn't do. Every night, every day, every morning. The first one
up town and the last one to go home . . . when I went home.
You never saw me sober, you hardly ever saw me sober. Had
those side burns, boy, way down to there . . . down there, had
'em down there, had a pretty black leather jacket with "Hell's
Lost Angels" on the back of it, you know. The leader of a gang,
more or less, supposed to be anyway. And I had a gang there.
The big black engineer boots on, the tight black dress pants,
sit around all the time, you know. Going in and throw myself
around. I felt I'd just made so much progress, man, I mean,
things like getting my hair cut and cutting those side-burns off,

dressing right and everything. It's just progress to me and saving my money and working and not drinking [unclear] and I got drunk. I just couldn't fight it. I was disappointed. Felt real bad about it. And now I'm actually, and no kidding, no, no joke about it, I just cry inside and I'm getting to realize what a mess it was, the things I done. I never had thought about—I hadn't even thought about them before.

The fifty-third hour:

And I never did, I had this feeling for people and everything, you know, but I never would show it as much as I should. I would always try to use people, when it came to money, after I learned the meaning of money, and what it can do for you, I always tried to get it anyway I could and if it meant hurting my best friend, I'd do that. And money, it was just money. Money came before anything else, to me. And I never did have much feeling when it came to that as I should. I never did have any what you might call thinking time, I never did think about these things. What I should have done was sat down and thought about it four or five years ago. After I'd made my first mistake, my second, my third and my fourth, if I'd have thought about it then, I'd have realized. But it took me till now to do it. But I still don't think now's too late. Oh, I mean I'm still young. I might look at myself, I feel I'm getting older, but I'm still young, there's no way around that. My life hasn't even begun yet. If my older years are like my younger years, I'm in trouble. I'm hell-bound and everything else, I'm gone. But I think you've got to have something to look forward to. And I don't live for other people, I live for myself, and the things that I want. I think that's what keeps me living and what might keep me going; I just live for myself. I, that's the way I am. I don't have anything else to live for. Some day I'll still be sort of a big man, you know, sort of way up there; some day I'll be something. I've always really tried to be something; it was always the wrong thing to be. And I think I faced up to the things I did and paid for them. I'm paying for it now. I've paid for it in ways that you can't explain, like no friends, and I paid for it in not having a home, and I paid for it in my probation. I just paid for it in—in just a lot of ways you couldn't think about. And I paid for it in the way I feel, now, of which the way six or seven months ago I wouldn't have felt about it; I would have ran; I would have took off to another state or something like that. And I paid for it now in the worst payment I think there is thinking about it and facing up to it, which is the worst way you can pay is having to change . . .

You see working every day for nothing and you've got nothing to look forward to. Crazy. Work to exist. I'm not even a damn person. What do I want to exist for? I'm crazy. I really believe that. I think there's something wrong with me. I do, I do, the stupidest of, of anybody walking. I've messed up so many damn times it's pitiful. Want me to tell you about it again? . . . They give me chance after chance after chance. I can't blame nobody for—I can't blame nobody but myself. There's something wrong with me. I never thought about it till now. Never even give it a second thought . . . I want to go to the jungle, that's where I want to go [pause]. I'm lonely, boy, I'm telling you I'm lonely. I'm just not used to this stuff. I want to do things. I got the chance to do them if I want 'em and I can't enjoy them any more. I know what it is I think. It's, I'm, I'm just used to being a big man, you know. I am, that's probably it. Nobody pays much attention—the girls they look at me . . . God damn. I've been screwed up for four years. I didn't know whether I was coming or going. I don't know what to do now. I, I don't know. I'm sick, man. Seems like I sort of want somebody to feel sorry for me, you know, but, but then again I don't. I guess I had fun last night for about one of the first times. Went to sleep on the front porch. Oh, yeah, we just did it for the hell of it. I felt happy yesterday, I felt happy all day long. Last night and I felt happy today. The reason so I just, sort of, you know, I was telling you about meeting a girl, I figured out that that was the reason. I don't know, I get set-ting around over here and I start thinking about all these damn things. Go nuts! I change completely when I get under this damn microphone. As long as I don't think about it, I'm all right. That's when a man said, I have any feeling of guilt. I never did think about it. I never did think about what I was doing to people.

In such a condition, Bill faced a dilemma. He could not force the insight to happen again and he could not return completely to what he was before the insight. Typically, he tried to have the insight again by going back to the place of the initial insight and repeating the same procedures as previously. Sometimes he attempted to capture the insight in his imagination. Also he began reading psychology books. But nothing really worked. He could neither return to what he was nor go forward. Consequently, he began to believe that "it [insight] is something which can happen only once to a human being like me." But he was wrong.

This "giving up" or "letting go" was exactly what was required. Then, at unexpected moments in the street, at work, or at the laboratory, he would feel at the edge of an insight again. But as he reached toward it, trying to obtain it with conscious effort, it disappeared. Gradually, through such experiences with disappearing insight, he learned that he could search for moments of expanded awareness but he could not command them to happen. Nor could he grasp the life he really wanted as a goal "out there," or "beyond," or "in the future" as though it were an object of an idea. His search was to make himself aware of that which was already present. Alan Watts (1958, p. 76) has suggested this:

The natural world . . . reveals its content, its fullness of wonder, when respect [for it] hinders us from investigating it in such a way as to shatter it to abstraction . . . If I must map the canyons and count the trees, I shall never enter into the sound of a hidden waterfall . . . To abstain is not to postpone the cold disillusionment of the true facts but to see that one arrives by staying rather than going, that to be forever looking beyond is to remain blind to what is here.

More specifically, Jung (1953, p. 287) has said, "It is not I who create myself, but rather I happen to myself." This does not at all mean that the person is completely passive or that there is no thinking. Rather, the mind is actively engaged in expanding its boundaries of awareness and understanding. The conceptual screens through which the person usually views his world are dropped or shifted so that even ordinary objects or situations of daily life may bring a new and exciting meaning.

On the forty-third meeting between Bill and the experimenter, the experimenter met him a few blocks from the laboratory. Following their usual greeting, they walked along silently toward the laboratory, which was located at one of the main intersections of the city. Suddenly Bill began crying silently. Tears came from his open eyes as they walked through the busy traffic. Outside the laboratory, Bill talked for a few minutes to the janitor of the building. Inside, he began his interview by saying:

This is my happiest day in Massachusetts. This is the happiest day, the last thirty minutes is the happiest day in Boston or I could say in my life, I don't know. Because I can explain all of it. And, I left the house, and I wasn't, I wasn't thinking about it; I really wasn't, I wasn't thinking about it; and I started looking at people, I started looking at people and places. I looked at the cleaners, of how the guy was making his living. I looked at the car lots of how the people were making the easy buck off of cars. I looked at a man who was petting a cat. The guy was petting the cat. He looked like he didn't have a care in the world—probably had a thousand. I looked at the empty buildings that were businesses and I thought, said to myself that guy didn't make it here, I says, but I bet he went some-where else and tried again. And I, I looked at all the businesses and all the people and I thought to myself. They made it and they didn't give up. And I walked along, and I think I reached two blocks down the street and I started crying. Happy tears, really happy tears! . . .

I saw the people that work in the factories, I saw the guys that had wives and I saw how happy they were and I knew,

I felt how much trouble they had, and I felt like I could help them and I helped a dozen, at least twelve people I know with a smile. I smiled at them and they smiled back. I looked at the car lots, and the guys that were making the easy dollar on the car lots and I thought how much they went through to get there. And I told you I looked at buildings that were empty that they went somewhere else where they could make it . . .,

And I want to tell you something that, that I never thought would happen to me. It feels great to be guilty; it feels great to be guilty and care for people. It really feels great to feel guilty, to, to know that I've hurt people so much and that I want to unhurt them and never hurt anybody else. And it feels great to be sorry for other people, and it feels great to be sorry for myself. Because, you remember the time that I, that I was downhearted and everything. That, that, those four days hurt me worse than I think ten years in prison could do. And I know you can. This thing is, is happening to me, and, and its something I, I'm not going to miss out on. I'm smart enough and I want to and I feel it and it's, it's something I pray for, that I, that I won't miss out on. It's something I love. This, to me, is more exciting; this is the excitement, this is the thing I've been looking for all my life. That's what I feel. The thing I've missed out on is to find myself and care and feel guilty and pray and, and not hurt anybody . . . But this is the only really good thing that's ever happened to me. And it's pushing me, it's pushing me, it's behind me, it's around me, it's in front of me, on top of me, on bottom, it's pushing me on as nothing has ever done before . . .

These tears were not tears of despair or weakness but tears of joy as the world, which was always present, became visible for the first time.

As of this writing Bill is in prison. After working approximately a year and a half in a nearby city as a bus boy and then a baker's helper, he returned to his home state to enlist in the army. Upon his arrival, he was arrested at the bus station on several outstanding warrants and given a two-year sentence with six months to be served in prison. Apparently, his philosophical discoveries remained with him. From prison he wrote:

Friendship is one of the greatest things that will ever happen to people, if they take it and understand it and reason with it before it is too late and life is gone. Not death, but the real life of friendship. To get the love before it is too late.

Is it really too late for me now? Life must go on but the past stays forever and ever. You think you love, hate, and cry but still the life goes on . . .

My heart aches for the prisoners here. They don't realize the part of life they are missing as I didn't 'till a while back.

At last I am getting close to the ones I really love, my family.

Philosophical discoveries cannot provide immunity from the law or compensate for foolish mistakes. They may even make serving time in prison much more difficult than previously. Fortunately, none of the other eight boys interviewed within this philosophical context have been returned to prison or reform school.

The interviewing by a psychologist. The psychologist's major approach to interviewing was psychoanalytic. Excerpts from his paper, "Experimenter-Subject Psychotherapy: A New Method of Introducing Intensive Office Treatment for Unreachable Cases" (Slack, 1960) indicate how his interviews began "non-directively" and were gradually shifted toward an analytic orientation.

During these first hours the experimenter makes little attempt to direct the conversation to emotionally laden areas. On the other hand, he does try to get at the facts as seen by the subjects. He listens to the subject's "story" about how he is put upon by the police, by parents who are "on his back," and so on. The experimenter unconditionally accepts the emotional message of the subject, although he may register disbelief at some of the subject's attempts to "con" him. For example, the subject will often tell the experimenter "whoppers" about his skills at sports, sex, and crime. The experimenter may register mild disbelief or may accept the lies as truth, but should avoid giving the subject the impression that he (the subject) is being accepted on the basis of the lies. The subject should feel he would be accepted in any case . . . (p. 250).

In the meantime, research goes on. The subject is paid to take diagnostic tests of a very intensive and complete sort. Long-term thematic apperception tests, for example, are given; in these tests the subject is asked to tell many stories about a single picture. We are in no hurry. The idea is to get as complete a picture of the subject as can be obtained; at the same time we are allowing the interpersonal relationship to mature and grow warmer . . . (p. 251).

The subject discovers that, perhaps for the first time in his life, another individual has taken a sincere interest in him and proved it in concrete ways. Just the mere fact that the experimenter can be counted on to be on time and to devote time and money to the subject—to really deliver the promised goods —starts to work some change in the attitudes and behavior of the subject. He begins to skip hours less and less frequently and only with more reasonable excuses. The hour starts to become a very important part of the subject's day; he moves other events around in order to show up on time. Furthermore, the subject is very likely to start giving indications of the development of that phenomenon *which is perhaps the single most outstanding feature of E-S psychotherapy—an extremely powerful, almost overwhelming positive "transference" or rapport with almost no negative manifestation* . . . (p. 253).

Once the transference has taken hold and attendance is really regular, the experimenter has a way to go before "therapy" can begin. He must give insight which is truly recognizable as such by the subject and which will therefore give the subject a clear idea of how the process of psychotherapy operates. The initial insights can be used as a model for future therapeutic work and the experimenter can use even a "shallow" interpretation as a prototype. When the situation becomes structured as a therapeutic one, the insight (and the attention and support of the experimenter) become reinforcers of the act of attending in and of themselves. The subject reports that he does not come "just for the money" (p. 254).

The effectiveness of this approach in producing analytic insight is suggested by excerpts from interviews with a boy, Frank, who was initially extremely hostile toward psychotherapy. Before employment by the laboratory, Frank had persistently refused treatment even at the threat of imprisonment. Frank was one of the first boys interviewed by the psychologist and he worked somewhat longer hours at the laboratory and was paid at a slightly higher rate than most of the boys subsequently employed by the project. He was interviewed one hour each day, five days a week, and did other work around the laboratory for at least another hour each day. Including bonuses, his wages averaged twenty-five dollars a week. Frank reclined on a standard analytic couch and faced the experimenter during most of the interviews. The following excerpts from these interviews cover approximately an eight-month period and are presented chronologically from the earliest to latest. They are selected from "Intensive Individual Interpersonal Interviews with a Young Offender" (Slack, 1959).

FRANK: I don't know what the fuck you can do. It's a rat race. You can't get in that kind of fucking life; you might as well stay where you belong. Stay where you fuckin' belong. Stay where I belong, with the regular fucking people. Just where I live, the block, that's all . . . the fucking guys, the ordinary Joe, Joe Truckdriver, Joe Factoryworker, Joe Worker, Joe Fuckin', Just Plain Joe, Joe Nobody . . .

EXPERIMENTER: You've tried?

FRANK: I've tried. Fuck it. Fuck it. Fuck it. These fuckin' people make me laugh. They say [sarcastically], "You can make good if you want to. You've got a mind of your own, and you can make good." What the fuck do *they* know about how to make good? What do they know? Where you going to go, where you going to turn? Hah! You think you can start hanging with guys that have heard of you and know what you were like, know what you've done, time and everything else? You think you can hang with them kind of guys? You feel the freeze all of a sudden. "Well, Jesus, we would like to invite you, but we're going *here* and un . . ." You know? What do they know, Charlie, what do they know? Will you tell me? What the fuck do they know; what's the sense of all this shit? So I was cut out one fuckin' way. Forget about it. Might as well . . . fuck it . . .

This [psychiatrist] was a *weird*-looking bastard. Just like a regular guy you see in the movies: bushy hair, thick glasses, mustache. His eyes looked like they went right through you. He was only there about fifteen or twenty minutes. Then he says, "If your mother and someone else's mother were in a room nude, which one would you have something to do with?" I was getting pissed off; I says, "*Your* mother." "Get out, get out, get out!" He blew his top, you know. I'm telling you, they asked you some weird shit. Thy asked do you have any diseases, and if you're guilty, and what are you in here for, and I tried to tell them, you know. I says, "What the hell's the sense of talking to you; you ain't going to believe me; you ain't going to get me out of here anyway." So, he says, "What's the charge?" I says, "I and D." He says, "What's that?" I says, "Idling and disorderly." All I was doing was asking a girl for a cigarette at a quarter to one in the morning, and I was just idling, so they locked me up, I guess—I don't know. Contributing to delinquency too. That was the other charge. I was only seventeen; the broad was sixteen, so how the hell am I contributing to delinquency, when I'm as myself? I couldn't figure it . . .

[Several months later] Well, this is my *own* fuckin' theory. I started thinking whether he [Freud] was right, what he said. And I don't know how fucking far I got, but this is as far as I got. I can go on from there but I took that time when I was come off my mother's breast, see . . . So what was the first thing that happened. I got a pacifier, or I got a nipple. Now from my mother I got love, in that form, and I got nourishment, milk.

See? I started thinking of that. So when she took me off breast feeding, I figured, where was I gonna get . . . I was still gonna get nourishment, but where was I gonna get that love? or something to substitute for that love? A baby's bottle, with the nipple on the end, or a pacifier. Then later on, unconsciously when the kid grows up,—a baby, you give him anything, and the first thing they do, they put it in their mouth . . .

We start arguing and all, on how he [father] brought us up, and I says, "Look it, Father, or so-called Father, the only words I ever heard out of your mouth, as far as you helping me out, is "rotten" and "black sheep." "What do you mean?" he says, 'I put clothes on your back, and I put food in your belly," and all that type of stuff, and I says, "Look, is love food in your belly, or clothes on your back? Love isn't them material things like that. Is love and understanding them things, Pa?" "What do you mean? What do you mean?" I says, "You can take a dog and feed it, and then later on kick the shit out of it. And that dog will probably still come to you, if you feed it, or if you throw it a piece of meat, it will still eat. But it will be afraid of you." He looked at me . . . "Blah, blah, blah," but he shut up for a fuckin' . . . He thought of it too. I says, "You haven't ever given me any kind of love." "What do you mean; what kind of love; what do you mean, love, love. No one gives any." Then he started talking about himself, so I shut up, see, and I listened. Ha, ha, ha.

EXPERIMENTER: No one gave him any, huh?

FRANK: He come over here when he was seventeen . . . That's probably why, you know? And I started thinking, you know, about the whole family, and shit like that . . . I mean we're all fuckin' *whacky* . . .

EXPERIMENTER: Maybe you helped him?

FRANK: I *did*. I started him thinking like that; then I turned around and says to him, "Pa, put it this way. When you were growin' up . . ." Then I put it this other way to him; I says, "Look, when I started going to school, *everyone else I knew* told me that it was the greatest move I ever made; I was finally smart enough to start realizing about *life*." Not going to sit here and have the thing going to go by you, and you can't say,

"Well, gee, I should have done this, or I should have done that." You ain't doing shit . . ." You know, to myself, so I says, "Everyone else told me that this going to school was the greatest thing . . ." I said, "I'm not doing it for anyone else; I'm doing it for *me*. I realize that I'm doing it for *me*. But you, the one I wanted the most to tell me, out of all them people, you turned around and said, "bullshit" and "baloney" and walked away. In other words, I was no good, and you were trying to make me feel rotten. I says, "Now tell me, Father, because if you went up to your mother when you was a kid my age and you told her that, how would *you* feel? If your mother or father just looked at you and said . . . Or, if you went up to your father, and your father just says, 'Aw, get out of here, you rotten black sheep.'" I says, "How would you feel?" He says, "Blah, blah, blah; I put clothes on your back; I fed you," and all this stuff . . . I says, "Yeah, Pa, you did all the material things you could possibly do. But that's not it. Where's the understanding part of it? If something was on my mind, a worry, you never asked me what I ever liked to do. Even to this day . . . You just used to go out and tell me, 'Go out and get a job and work.' You didn't ask me whether I liked that job, or why don't I try this or that, or try to understand me. No. You used to just come in, and the only time you'd talk to me was when I'd done something wrong, and all you'd say was 'black sheep' or 'no good, rotten.'" He walked away . . . I could see his eyes swelling up though. Then I felt like a fuckin' rotten bastard. This shit can be dangerous too, if you don't use it right. So then I had to do something. So I went back in, and I says, "Hey, it's still not too late," and I patted him on the back. I didn't get none of them things when I was a kid, you know, so I patted him on the back, and I says, "I'm still here. I still need some understanding." You'd be surprised, man. Like I say, this guy Freud . . .

See, my old man, more or less, he took it for granted that I was getting all the love I needed, whereas, as far as he was concerned, his kind of love was material things. Like food and clothes on my back or food in my belly. But it wasn't. You need understanding, which is a form of love. Love is made up of many things, understanding, you got to be sympathetic, all this. Know what I mean? If a kid went and fucked up, you just don't go out and give him a fuckin', *but* that ain't going to prove a thing. That isn't going to prove nothing. In fact, it's dangerous. I've been thinking about this all week.

EXPERIMENTER: I didn't tell you about this.

FRANK: I know.

EXPERIMENTER: But it's right.

Following this new insight into his behavior, Frank began applying psychoanalytic theory to many aspects of his daily life. He reported to the experimenter a particularly illustrative incident of his use of free association in the barroom. This incident might be subtitled, "Therese and the Bongos":

FRANK: . . . And I was talking to this girl . . . I says, "Geeze, Therese, you appear to be an awful lot rejected." I said, "What are you? You look like a depressed." She says, "Ohhh, I'm not . . ." She was beating on this drum, you know?

EXPERIMENTER: On a drum?

FRANK: Yeah, she was beating on this little bongo drum in the club. She was one of them Lithuanian broads that always hang around and all. They're intelligent bastards, girls too. So I says to ———, the kid beside me, "Watch this." S———'s sitting there, saying, "Oh man, dig man . . ." And suddenly I see a little bit of myself through the way he acts, his actions, you know? "Dig man" and all this shit. And it seems so . . . I felt like going over and smacking him, and, you know, just get a book by Freud or something, or common sense, and pour it into his fuckin' head. But, uh, it takes a long time to think of all this shit. But, a—a, you see—you see how ridiculous it was, you know, the way you're acting. So I says to the girl anyway, you know, I says, "Gee, you seem awfully depressed." She says, "What do you mean?" I says, "Well, I noticed something must be on your mind; you're doing a terrible job on them bongo drums." She's beating it and beating it and beating it, like that. *That's* where I connected the ideas with the thoughts and the actions, you know? All of a sudden I found out she stopped. And in my own mind I'd said, she *will* stop, pretty soon. And she *did*. She stopped, and she says, "What do you mean?" I says, "I'll bet I can read your mind. I'll bet I can bring out something that you're worrying about." She says, "What are you, some kind of a witch-doctor," or, like I said, fortune teller or something like that. I says, "No." I played that free association. I said, "Well, you got to be honest with me." You can tell when a person's not honest, you know what I mean? They'll think of the thought; they'll blink their eyes, and they'll go, "Uh . . . uh . . . uh," and they'll try to think of another thought, and they've forced it back into their subconscious. Or it's trying to pierce the subconscious, but it gets fucked up in between the conscious and the subconscious.

EXPERIMENTER: I don't know how you've come out with all this stuff; *I* never told you any of this . . .

FRANK: I tell you, when I'm interested in something . . . I just didn't want to come up here and "Charlie Slack: therapist ———— ————: subject:" I want to know what's going on before I'll play the game, ha ha.

EXPERIMENTER: So what happened with the bongo?

FRANK: So, I says water; she says drink, see? So then I says, what the fuck did I say? In other words, I come a round-about way of it . . . I says water; she says drinking. I says knife; she says fork. I says plate; she says, you eat, or something like that. Then I says boy; she says Paul, instead of saying girl. See? So then I knew. Somewhere along the line . . . *Paul*, see? So then I got off the track again, purposely . . . You got to have a little bit of the element of surprise in there, a little bit, the way you put the thought. But if I just said Paul, and I didn't say anything, she'd start thinking, so she wouldn't talk to me anymore. She'd know what my thoughts were. So I says boy; she says Paul. Then right away I says mother; she says father. I says love; she says Paul. So then I stopped, and I says, "Well, look it, Therese, my advice to you . . ."

EXPERIMENTER: Ha, ha, ha. Go back with Paul.

FRANK: It's only common sense, really, when you come down to it. So I says, so all the other ones are looking surprised, so then I says, all right, see? So everything was fast, the words, the way I was doing it. So then I says, "Well, my advice to you is, I don't know how the argument started, I don't know who left who, but I says for yourself, I says, you should get with Paul, I says, and compromise, and come to some kind of . . . condition." "How did you know? How did you know?" And even S——— looks up, and he says, "Oh man, you've been talking to Charlie too much." I looked up and I felt like smacking him one. I tried to get him you know; he's going to be my favorite subject, that fuckin' S———. I'll cure that bastard's mind, or I'll get him thinking, if it's the last thing I do. I can see why *you're* interested in this shit. *Believe* it, *believe* it. Everything I do now, I . . . (Slack, 1959, pp. 17–18).

Frank's involvement with analytic theory soon led to his being isolated from his friends who could not understand such "weird" thoughts. He then gave up "thinking about psychology," and regained some of his old friends. His participation in illegal activities has noticeably decreased with the exception of one court appearance for the unauthorized use of his brother-in-law's car. He is presently married and working as a laborer for a construction company. It is now over three years since his initial analytic insight and he reports that he is again getting somewhat interested in psychology, but in a calmer manner, because "Freud is still right."

The interviewing by a social worker and social work student. These experimenters conducted interviews from a psychiatric case work approach which tended to focus on a boy's relation to his immediate environment.

In discussions among the experimenters, they often stressed the importance of working with a total situation made up of the individual interacting with his environment. This therapeutic orientation resulted in the experimenter's efforts being directed toward the individual or his environment or toward both simultaneously. In one case, the experimenter provided a boy with money for room rent after his mother had angrily asked him to leave home. Before giving him the money, however, the experimenter had a lengthy interview with the boy about his feelings toward his mother. Also, the experimenter would occasionally accompany a boy to various employment agencies to help him find a job.

In stressing the need for direct intervention in the boy's environment, the social worker wrote with Dr. Slack the following suggestion:

Although Experimenter-Subject research is an independent experimental activity, at some points it may be advisable for the experimenter to seek to alleviate certain external conditions which militate against the growth and development of the delinquent into a mature person and a good citizen. The young offender, with his criminal record, has trouble in getting good employment and in joining social activities of a new sort. The close relationship between experimenter and subject as well as the wealth of data collected from the subject may enable the experimenter to obtain a fairly accurate idea of whether the subject has changed in his attitudes and behavior sufficiently to deserve a "break" as far as a good job goes. To help him get this job, cooperation from local labor unions, trade associations, business groups, etc., will have to be achieved (Slack and Kantor, 1959, p. 4).

Much of the work done by the social worker and social work student as experimenters would fit very well into traditional social work practice. There was always, however, the important difference that the delinquents were not like usual social work clients because they were being paid.

The interviewing by a priest. The priest stated his objectives in interviewing as "letting the boy talk, helping

him to understand himself, and working with his parents."
For the first several weeks, his interviews with a boy would
be essentially nondirective. Gradually the interviews would
become more directive. In their final form, after several
months, an interview would usually begin in a nondirective
manner and end in a directed discussion of the church's
position on various topics selected by the boy. Since the
priest was often involved in religious matters, it was felt
that the presentation of him as a priest would be the most
honest procedure in this situation. For this reason, he wore
clerical garb while working at the laboratory.

The priest interviewed only Roman Catholic boys and
among these boys the combination of experimental and
priestly characteristics greatly facilitated the initial relation. They immediately tended to relate to him as a "good"
man and at the same time use him as an enjoyable target
for their hostility toward the church and middle-class moral
standards. Thus, while being overtly polite by getting up
to offer him a seat or addressing him as "Father," they
would at the same time deliberately ask him embarrassing
questions in the presence of other boys, such as, "Is it
wrong to masturbate?". Much laughter and lively discussion
would follow. In group meetings which the experimenter
led, this type of discussion was raised at times to the level
of a "sport." The opportunity for just this "sport" alone
could have been enough to guarantee attendance.

Under the conditions described above, rapport was
quickly established. For example, after three weeks, Len, a
19-year-old, wrote for the experimenter at the experimenter's request his opinion about the project:

I have been a part, material wise, in the program at Harvard
University, titled "Research Center in Personality and Rehabilitation" for a period of 3 weeks. The person in that department I work with is———[the experimenter]. Who is a

Jesuit priest finishing a degree in Sycology at this University. Now the main purpose of this program is to get material and also at the same time, help troubled people who have delinquently dealt with the law, who naturally have many different types of problems. Myself being a person under that description can be of use to this program. I must honestly state, that in my such short period attending here so far, I have never since I can remember, felt greater mentaly. Although it has only been a short period of time, as I mentioned, I feel a great decrease in my trouble with facing reality. I hope it is possible for me to continue my attendance for quite awhile. Because I still have much more information to give to this program about myself, and different things. I also feel there is much more knowing I can receive about myself here. I have, as most troubled people, always thought that I would never straiten things out. But now since attending these visits I have put a whole new light on everything concerning life and myself. And the light is on the good side, one hundred per cent. After finding this information out on such a short visit here, I am sure enough of everything, to say that the outcome of this will be excellent, not only for me but everyone else that attends this program. If this program was greatly increased I feel both sides would benefit greatly. I hope I have expressed myself as well as I wanted to about this matter.

In the excerpt above, the boy's initial perceptions of the project involve a strong therapeutic overtone. He mentions "troubled people," "problems," and "facing reality." Gradually, however, his orientation was shifted to religious concerns as indicated by an excerpt from a letter written to the experimenter by this boy four months later:

I suspect things would be ideal if I went to church. I haven't gone since I was a kid because there's just no meaning there to it.

Everyone could go to some kind of chapel meeting at [reform school] where I was unless they were locked up in isolation.

They called it chapel but it wasn't church. It was dark in the back there and the guys would pass stuff and the faggots would giggle and make out.

Maybe my trouble started when I quit church and everything —Everything, you know, that in some sense goes along with church like respect and family and things.

Eventually, a nearby church where the experimenter worked became a secondary focus of interest for the boys in the project. One boy, Walter, after a night of exceptionally heavy drinking, went to the church at 2:30 in the morning to share his troubles with the experimenter. But the experimenter was not there and the church was locked. When the experimenter arrived in the morning, the boy was asleep on the front steps. The police had not bothered him as they usually would have. For him, the church had become something of a medieval sanctuary.

The visits of the experimenter to the homes of the boys he interviewed combined priestly authority with, usually, intercession on behalf of the boy. The experimenter reported to the laboratory one particularly successful visit to the home of a boy who refused to get a job. The boy's mother would send him out early in the morning to find a job. Before sending him out, however, she would strongly remind him that the family needed his room and board money. [His mother had started to charge him fifteen dollars a week for room and board and he owed at this point over one hundred dollars according to her calculations.] The boy's attitude was "Why work? Uncle Sam and the family will take it all anyway." After leaving the house in the morning, he would promptly head for a bar in town to help clean it and to "loosen up" on a few beers. He would then proceed to an early morning pool room, then to the bowling alley, and finally arrive at a motorcycle shop where he would stay until early afternoon. Eventually, he would return home to announce that he was unable to find a job. Sometimes he would have his friends at the pool room or motorcycle shop call home to imitate a prospective employer. But, of course, since he was not at home he was unable to get the "job" offered by his friends.

When the experimenter visited this boy's mother, he told her quite clearly that if she wanted her son to get a job she would have to stop trying to force him to find one. Further, the boy should not be obligated to pay for room and board as long as he was unemployed. When he was working, he could contribute some of his money to the family, but not all of it. He should have some money for himself. Very shortly after this, the boy reported that things were "going better" at home. Within the following month he had a full-time job in the shipping department of a large store.

When officially visiting the homes of the boys, the experimenter operated within the role of priest. Experimenter-priest would best describe the priest's role throughout the project.

2. Secondary Activities

The primary activity of the project was interviewing as described above. However, as the project progressed, secondary activities were derived largely from the suggestions of the boys themselves. Although the specific nature of these secondary activities varies widely, they were designed with two objectives in mind: 1) the activity was to involve both the experimenter and subject in a mutually important task, and 2) the activity itself was to be effective in reducing crime. Some of the major secondary activities are discussed here; others are presented in Part II.

One of the most popular secondary activities was the programmed rewriting of the *Driver's Handbook*. Auto theft was one of the most frequent offenses of the delinquents employed by the project. An exploratory study suggests a causal situation something like this. The boy tries to borrow a car for a date or to drive around because he feels restless, but, because he has no driver's license, he cannot borrow a car. Consequently, he steals one for temporary use and then abandons it in a nearby town. A car is very rarely sold, stripped, or deliberately wrecked.

Assuming, for the purpose of experimentation, that there was a relation between auto theft and the possession of a driver's license, a secondary activity was begun to help the boys get licenses. This involved getting permission from the parole officer for the boy to have a license, teaching him how to drive, and helping him learn the *Massachusetts Driver's Handbook* (a manual for passing the written part of the state's examination). Most of the boys considered the written part of the examination the most difficult part. They were unsure of their ability to pass it, and afraid of being laughed at by the other fellows if they failed.

To change this situation, seven boys (without licenses and with a record of auto thefts) were asked to help rewrite a driver's training manual. This rewriting or "programming" consisted largely of rewriting the *Driver's Handbook* so that it was broken down into small, easy-to-learn steps. In its final form, certain important information from the *Driver's Handbook* was printed on 3″ × 5″ cards, which the boy was to read. Then he was asked to answer a question about the information he read by filling in a blank on this same card. By turning the card over, he could know immediately whether his answer was correct or not. If incorrect, he would have to study the card again. If correct, he could go on to the next card. The language and questions became increasingly difficult until they exactly corresponded to the language and questions in the *Driver's Handbook*. A thorough memorization of answers from this programmed handbook could guarantee passing the written section of the driver's examination. Using this procedure the boys were able to learn the *Handbook* without embarrassment and at their own rate.

All seven boys were able eventually to get licenses. Only one, after getting his license, was involved in larceny of an automobile. It is reported that he and two friends got into an argument with a cab driver late one Saturday night over the fare they were being charged. They refused to pay; the driver insisted. Finally, they gave the driver a five-dollar bill, pushed him out of the cab, and announced they were taking the cab for "change." They were soon apprehended by the police in a neighboring town where they were randomly offering people free rides. Although the other six boys working on the driver's manual were not subsequently involved in automobile offenses, the sample is too small to confirm conclusions regarding the effectiveness of this procedure in reducing auto theft.

Another popular secondary activity were the group meetings at the laboratory. They were led by the priest and occasionally by the psychologist with usually five to eight boys in attendance. (Two or three of these boys were also employed in other activities of the project.) All of the members of the group were twenty-one years old or over. As an incentive for attendance, beer was served at the beginning of the meeting and each participant was given a dollar at the end. Each meeting lasted one hour and when it was over, the group would often leave together for a bar to continue their discussion.

The priest led the group meetings in very much the same manner as he conducted individual interviews. The following excerpts come from a group meeting which included two prospective members. These excerpts are typical of many meetings but do not contain the intense personal interactions present in some. After approximately ten minutes of refreshments and general confusion, the priest began the discussion by getting a new member and his friend to sit at the table. (The following excerpts are from initial transcriptions by the author of tape recordings no longer available.)

EXPERIMENTER: Come to the table.

KARL: We like it over here.

EXPERIMENTER: No, come to the table.

KARL: What about the voice? [Tape recording]

EXPERIMENTER: No, don't worry about the voice, it cannot be used without your permission. You have to give it for that.

KARL: It can't?

EXPERIMENTER: No, unless you give your permission. Don't feel bad about that. I feel bad seeing you behind me.

KARL: I'll sit over here.

EXPERIMENTER: Yes, please sit there.

KARL: Can I speak in Polish?

EXPERIMENTER: Yes, you may speak in Polish . . . [Laughter]

LEN: Where's the beer?

NEAL: All gone.

LEN: All gone?

NEAL: It's in the ice box. [Hands Len a can of beer.]

LEN: It's warm, it's warm.

WALT: What's the matter? Didn't you ever drink warm beer before?

EXPERIMENTER: I put this beer in the refrigerator last Friday. Maybe somebody took it out.

LEN: God damn, I know that refrigerator wasn't on! [Laughter]

The discussion continued in this manner for several minutes then the priest began again:

EXPERIMENTER: Any topics?

WALT: Put it [the beer] in the refrigerator.

EXPERIMENTER: Hey Len!

LEN: Yeah?

EXPERIMENTER: How about some topics for today?

LEN: Neal, what about a topic?

NEAL: I don't know, I don't know.

EXPERIMENTER: We've run out of things to talk about? Dan?

DAN: What the hell does everyone pick on me for? Shit! Pick on him [Sam]: he's . . .

EXPERIMENTER: I'm not picking on you, but it is the first time for them, and I feel the ones who have been here longer know better.

LEN: That's right . . .

SAM: Let's talk about falling hair or something.

EXPERIMENTER: It's up to you. I don't want to make any suggestions.

WALT: Let's see who can drink the most. Would you [Sam] like a beer?

EXPERIMENTER: The ice is coming, I hope . . .

WALT: What would you [Sam] do with a million dollars?

SAM: A million dollars—it'd take you a lifetime to spend it . . .

WALT: [To Neal] What would you do with a million dollars?

NEAL: I know one thing, I wouldn't go to heaven. [Looking at the experimenter.]

EXPERIMENTER: [With anger] I'm not a priest here!

WALT: Buy your own soul to heaven; right, Father?

EXPERIMENTER: What?

WALT: Buy your own soul to heaven.

For the next twenty minutes the group discussed ways to use a million dollars. The suggestions were to buy horses, travel, pay bills, and buy brass knuckles for the nuns at a local school. The discussion then shifted to describing incidents of misbehavior in school. There was agreement, finally, that you learn most at a strict school. Toward the end of the hour, one of the fellows interrupted the small talk to ask whether anyone present had an Oedipus complex. After a few humorous remarks, the meeting finally ended with the two prospective members deciding that they had enjoyed the group and wanted to join. The group voted to accept them.

In the secondary activity called "multiple interviewing," one subject was interviewed alternately by three interviewers who had widely different theoretical backgrounds.

Interviewer A would interview the boy on Monday, interviewer B on Wednesday, and interviewer C on Friday. All interviews were held at three o'clock in the afternoon in the same room; they were forty minutes in length, and were recorded. The experimenters did not discuss the interviews among themselves. The student in education, also an interviewer, supervised the experiment, edited the tapes, and evaluated the progress. The experiment was continued for four months until the boy left for the service.

The results obtained by each of the three interviewers were strikingly different. Interviewer A, the student in education, conducted nondirective interviews. Interviewer B, a third-year medical student, conducted interviews from a psychiatric orientation. Interviewer C, a Harvard undergraduate junior who had no previous experience in interviewing, was allowed to interview in any manner he wished. The interviews with interviewer C could be described as friendly discussions or "bull sessions," centering around girls, crime, sports, religion, and motorcycles. Very often following these interviews, interviewer C and the boy would play pool, work on the experimenter's motorcycle, or go bowling. These outside activities were permitted with the understanding that they would be announced ahead of time and open to visits by members of the project of interested persons. Eventually some of these outside meetings were filmed and recorded.

The following three excerpts may suggest the wide range of response of this boy to the various interview techniques. All of the excerpts are taken from the first fifteen minutes of the seventh interview with each interviewer.

JOHN: . . . So my parole officer is going before the Board sometime this month and get my parole dismissed so I'll be off parole and everything then and get my license the last two weeks or something I'm here.

INTERVIEWER A: Sounds as though it went pretty good for you.

JOHN: Huh?

INTERVIEWER A: Went pretty good for you.

JOHN: Yeah, it did, 'cause it was, the record was pretty bad and the judge didn't think he should dismiss it, but he did. He gave me a break . . . [Long pause, boy rubs eye.]

INTERVIEWER A: What's the matter with your eye?

JOHN: No, got something in it. [Drinks coke.] Well, what else we going to talk about? [Pause, no response from the interviewer.] Oh yeah, last Monday we went in town, we went in town looking for a job, me and the other kid did, the one you seen me with, so we started looking for a job, you know, and we didn't get a job so we're walking around town. We sees these three broads you know, they look kind of like pick-ups, you know. They weren't too clean, or anything like that, kind of dirty skirts and everything. So we followed them a little ways . . . [Describes the three girls as runaways from a correctional home about eighty miles away. They take the girls to his friend's home, let them have a bath, and have a "little fun" with them. They then borrow some clothes for the girls and finally leave them stranded at a restaurant.)

INTERVIEWER A: Pretty rough on them, ha?

JOHN: Yeah. One broad only had two months and she would have got out. Crazy!

INTERVIEWER A: Not too smart then.

JOHN: No, really stupid. Two months is nothing.

INTERVIEWER B: Could you say something more about your family than you've already told me?

JOHN: Well, they came up to visit me every Sunday at the reform school, but they didn't tell anyone where I was, like my aunt and uncle. They didn't want anyone to find out. They each came alone on visiting Sunday. My mother came one Sunday and my father the next. But my father didn't come much because he works some Sundays. So no one would notice they were gone.

INTERVIEWER B: Your father didn't want to see you as badly as your mother. [Long pause.]

JOHN: He had to work. He works at the ———. They make

———— and things like that. They're one of the biggest places like that and they almost had a strike a little while ago. My dad's on the union.

INTERVIEWER B: He's a big, important man.

JOHN: He's a big man there sort of. He's been there a long time and then there was almost a strike and he handled it.

INTERVIEWER B: He handles things around home too?

JOHN: He's not there a lot of the time so we run things by ourselves. [Pause] I'm taller than he is already.

INTERVIEWER C: What do you think of Ralph [Interviewer A]?

JOHN: Oh, he's . . .

INTERVIEWER C: Don't be afraid to . . . this, this is my tape, you know, and he won't get it. What'd you think? [difficulty with recording] Yea, there we go. So what, oh, what were we talking about, Ralph?

JOHN: Yea, what I thought of Ralph. I don't think you got it on the tape yet, did you?

INTERVIEWER C: No, try it again.

JOHN: I thought he was queer. I didn't think he was going to do, do this here [referring to the interviewing] for nothing, you know. What'd you think of him?

INTERVIEWER C: Well . . . what'd, what'd he say to you at first, you know, when you first met him?

JOHN: Well, he was, ah, he asked me where I'd been and all that, you know. How many times I went to court and all that. I thought that was, that's the way, you know, a queer usually plays up to you like that, you know . . . [more difficulty with the recording].

INTERVIEWER C: Why, a lot, a lot of guys that are queers around here? This is what I've heard. I've heard that, that, ah . . .

JOHN: Yes.

INTERVIEWER C: [Offers the boy some potato chips.] Go ahead.

JOHN: No thanks.

INTERVIEWER C: I've heard that they, that a lot of guys in order to eat and everything live off them.

JOHN: Yeah.

INTERVIEWER C: They go that far, is that right?

JOHN: Yeah, they call it hustling queers, that's what they call it. Make a lot of money that way. You know what I mean? There's a lot of kids that hustle them but sooner or later you turn queer yourself. You know, you go around the —, that's a place you should go in. Some night drop in the —. You know where it is?

INTERVIEWER C: No . . . [John describes the location of the bar.] What'd these queers have a lot of money?

JOHN: Oh, yeah.

INTERVIEWER C: What'd they work or—?

JOHN: There's a lot of them, lot of them are rich, you know what I mean, they come from nice families, you know, rich families. They, they're just not right. They've got the mind of a girl; but physically they're a man, you know, mentally they're a girl and physically they're—. Like, ah, you go in the—, if you didn't, if, I guess if you didn't know that the waitresses were really men, you know, I mean you'd really—

INTERVIEWER C: Dressed up like women?

JOHN: Yeah.

INTERVIEWER C: Are you shitting?

JOHN: No, I'm not shitting you, I'm telling you, you go in there and see how they put up, put on their make-up. You'd never see a broad that could put on make-up as good as they do, I'm not shitting you. They really do it good. And they, and they wear perfume and tight pants, you know, slacks.

INTERVIEWER C: . . . [Interviewer tells story in which a New York chorus line surprises the audience at the end of the show by being men. Both laugh loudly.]

For the first few weeks, certain stories were repeated almost identically for each experimenter. Then, gradually, the content broadened so that it, as well as the general tone, varied according to each interviewer's orientation. For example, analytic terms that were commonly used by the boy during interviews with interviewer B were infrequently used during interviews with interviewers A and C. Also, the positive feelings of the boy toward each interviewer developed at a different rate and appeared to be of a different type for each interviewer. A positive relation was most rapidly established between the boy and interviewer C, the undergraduate student, and least rapidly with interviewer B, the psychiatrically oriented medical student. The feeling of the boy toward interviewer A might be best characterized as "personal trust," toward interviewer B as "therapeutic-dependence," and toward interviewer C as "friendly admiration." The sudden arrival of these three interviewers as new, psychologically important people in his life apparently had considerable impact. After the first few weeks of interviewing, the boy got a part-time job with a chair rental company which he held for several months before going into the service.

Throughout the duration of the experiment, four months, the boy continually attempted to play the experimenters against each other to his own advantage—sometimes successfully. There is some indication that success in changing the boy's behavior by one experimenter was seen as a challenge by the others. The experimenters did not know each other except for one meeting prior to the experiment, and moderate hostility developed. A mutual working together by the experimenters was not attempted.

Four months is actually too short a period to evaluate the results in terms of traditional "therapeutic" procedures. However, even within these limitations, the boy was able to tolerate the ambiguity, form a close relation with each of the experimenters, and did not get into further legal difficulty. Additional investigation of multiple interviewing now seems feasible. It should proceed, however, with closer attention to the relations among the interviewers.

Another secondary activity was interviewing in a church setting. One of the primary reasons for selecting a church setting was to test the strength of the project's procedures in gaining attendance and cooperation. As mentioned before, several boys who were previously employed by the project were asked which places they would be least likely to go. They agreed on two places: a church and a police station. Of these two places, the church seemed more expedient. It was hoped that the boys might become familiar with the church and eventually learn to use its resources when they needed help.

The experimenter and his assistants, one graduate student and two undergraduates, were very inaccurate in predicting the difficulties in this experiment. The first unexpected major problem was that of finding a church willing to cooperate. While most churches agreed that the church should help reduce delinquency two concrete objections were usually raised: 1) Much church property was already being damaged or stolen. With delinquents in the church this damage would probably increase. 2) The young girls of the congregation would be subjected to an unwholesome influence from these boys. To meet these two objections, the project offered to guarantee that no boy would walk through the church unless accompanied by a person from the project, and that the boys would not attend any youth activities of the church. If the church committee was still reluctant, its final objection to cooperating with such a project was generally that "the church is a place for believers."

After nearly two months of searching, a church was found which would allow the project to use the church library. The church committee appointed a subcommittee to oversee the project. This subcommittee consisted of the minister of Christian education, an attorney who was an ex-policeman, and the director of a research organization in physical chemistry. This provided an excellent interdisciplinary background for the subcommittee in recognition of the fact that this was one of the few times, perhaps the first, that a church had housed a psychological laboratory for experimental research.

The second difficulty that the experimenters had not expected was the *enthusiastic* attendance of the delinquents. Since a Protestant church was being used, only Protestant boys were employed in this particular activity. However, in order to get into the experiment, several boys of a different religious orientation claimed to be Protestant. One boy succeeded for several weeks before the experimenter discovered he was Catholic. With some embarrassment, the experimenter obtained permission from the local priest for the boy to continue.

The boys were met on the street and offered the job of experimental subject as described previously. To avoid prejudicing the results regarding the effectiveness of this employment procedure, these boys were selected from sections of Cambridge where the project was unknown. As usual, the boys thought the job offer was part of a "con game" or a joke. When they were told that the psychological laboratory was in a church, they were sure something was "phony." A characteristic question was, "What are you, some new kind of a nut?" The experimenter would continue to explain that the laboratory did not have anything to do with the church activities. There was no obligation to attend church and they would not be preached at. Also, they were reassured that there were no police inside without uniforms. Their job would be talking into a tape recorder. Finally, they were encouraged to bring a friend along and look over the situation. Perhaps because the situation involved money, experimentation, a church, and intrigue, the offer to look over the situation was almost irresistible in comparison to the boredom of standing on the corner. On one occasion, an experimenter reported being greeted jokingly by the comment, "Hey, what's this

—the Salvation Army gone modern?" But the boy came along.

Eventually, the eagerness of the boys to have their friends participate in the project created a new problem. When a boy brought his friends along to the church, they would usually wander through the church until he was finished. The project had neither the personnel nor the room to engage these boys in other activities. Some of these boys began hiding and playing cards in the large subbasement of the church, which was made up of partially excavated rooms somewhat reminiscent of catacombs. When they were asked why they were hiding in the basement, one boy replied, "What cop would think of looking for a kid in a church?" Thus, the boys had turned the church into an excellent hideout.

This problem was brought to the attention of the church committee. Does this church have an "open door" policy regarding the use of church property for activities other than worship or will certain people be excluded? The decision was made to exclude friends of the subjects, except on the few occasions when there would be group interviews including friends. Ironically, then, the project was faced with the job of reducing delinquent attendance rather than increasing it. When the boys were told about this decision, they grumbled briefly about "wierdos" and "faggots" in the church but did not return or cause damage to church property.

Inside the church building, the boys generally expressed their anger toward the church by making noise or by trying to shock the church members with their "badness." For example, particularly angry glances were exchanged one Thursday afternoon between two boys and the Women's Fellowship Work Group. The Fellowship Group was having luncheon and discussing plans for a Christmas bazaar. The boys, in their usual motorcycle attire, scuffled several times through the room where the women were meeting. Finally, one woman asked facetiously, "Do you boys happen to be interested in our work?" The answer was, "Yeah." The woman then explained that they were starting to collect gifts for the treasure table at the Christmas bazaar. They collect toys, pottery, jewelry, clothes, and so forth. What they don't sell at the bazaar they give to the needy to help them have a nice Christmas. To this, one of the boys replied, "Well, what we need we'll just take!" and hurried out of the room before breaking into guffaws of laughter. Fortunately, encounters of this nature were infrequent. When they did occur, the boys seemed to enjoy the added excitement. Both members and delinquents eventually adjusted to a peaceful, but separate, use of the church property (Schwitzgebel and Covey, 1963b).

At the same time that interviews were being conducted in the church, one of the most popular secondary activities in our usual laboratory was the building of electronic equipment. This activity began rather accidentally when several boys were asked to help repair a tape recorder. The equipment which they built consisted largely of tape recorders and hi-fi sets built from kits purchased by the project and small, incidental equipment. One boy built a gadget which would cook a hot dog within two minutes by running 110 volts directly through it. Another boy helped build a transistorized, mobile loudspeaker system which fitted under the hood of a car. With it, the driver could talk to pedestrians along the road while driving.

This "building" usually consisted of following detailed directions for wiring the components together. The experimenters were surprised to discover how little these working-class boys knew about electronic principles. The boys required close supervision in order to avoid extensive damage to the equipment. For example, the boy who was helping to build the loudspeaker system was asked to solder the cord of a microphone onto a radio jack. Since the boy knew how to solder, the experimenter left him alone to complete the job. When the experimenter returned in about fifteen minutes, the boy said to him, "I don't think it'll work." When the experimenter asked why, the boy explained that smoke had come out of the microphone. When asked how that had happened, the boy explained that he had plugged the microphone directly into the wall socket to see if he could talk to someone.

The next day the boy was assigned the same soldering job with a similar microphone. The experimenter did not leave the room this time, but when he checked the boy's work, he found him meticulously unraveling the paper insulation from around the wires inside the cord. Since the boy could see no good reason for the paper, he decided that the factory had made a mistake. The experimenter was persistent. He explained that it was usually a good idea to assume that the factory was right until after the equipment was tested. Finally, the job was completed with the third microphone and the equipment installed in the car. Several days later when the experimenter went out to his car, he found the boy "improving" the microphone. The inside parts of the microphone were distributed over the dashboard while the boy was "just adding a piece of tinfoil to something down there in them little guts."

As a secondary activity, instead of using a standard interviewing technique, the psychologist played cards with three of the subjects. These card games were regularly scheduled for an hour, two to three times a week. The boys were paid two dollars an hour. The usual games were Gin Rummy or Five-Hundred.

While this card playing was a highly valued activity among the delinquents, it also provided the experimenter with an excellent opportunity to work with the boys' patterns of cooperation, competition, and impulsiveness. It was also an excellent vehicle for expressing affection, anger, dominance, submission, trust, and so forth. For example, the display of affection in the following excerpt would probably not have occurred in a direct face-to-face conversation. It is as though the boy and the experimenter allow their feelings to be expressed through the indirectness or "cover" of the card game.

GEORGE: What're we playing, Five Hundred?

EXPERIMENTER: [Nods yes] . . . Five, six, seven.

GEORGE: Deal one more. I'm first, right?

EXPERIMENTER: Right.

GEORGE: Any donuts left?

EXPERIMENTER: Yep . . . [brings box over and the boy helps himself; game continues.]

GEORGE: I got it! I got it! I got it! Got a nine. Rummy here and Rummy here. [Putting down cards.]

EXPERIMENTER: No!

GEORGE: You can do it!

EXPERIMENTER: No, you've got to pick up the whole thing!

GEORGE: Fuck you. [Laughing.]

EXPERIMENTER: You've got to take it all, you don't . . .

GEORGE: Fuck you.

EXPERIMENTER: Go saying, "Rummy."

GEORGE: Fuck you, fuck you. [Boy puts card back.]

EXPERIMENTER: "Rummy, Rummy, Rummy" like that. [Both laugh.] You can't do that. [Game continues.]

GEORGE: Yeah, here's a king for me . . . Another king, another king. Another one like that. Another one. Another one, Charl. Charl, one more. Beautiful, Charlie.

EXPERIMENTER: Here's your three if you want it . . . None of that last play crap either. [Game continues, both whistling.]

The following excerpt may illustrate how interviewing technique and interpretation was woven around the mechanics of a game.

EXPERIMENTER: All right [unclear].

GEORGE: I'm hungry.

EXPERIMENTER: Eat another one. [The boy is offered a donut and some lemonade.]

GEORGE: I am.

EXPERIMENTER: Eat juice, it's good for you.

GEORGE: No.

EXPERIMENTER: It's good for you.

GEORGE: What?

EXPERIMENTER: Vitamins.

GEORGE: Oh yeah, I'm going to have some later on [unclear]. I didn't get no sleep.

EXPERIMENTER: Why?

GEORGE: Good thing I got out of the house yesterday, man.

EXPERIMENTER: What happened?

GEORGE: I didn't stay and sleep. My old man came home from work sick. ["Sick" means drunk. Both the boy and his father are heavy drinkers.]

EXPERIMENTER: Oh yeah?

GEORGE: And he's sick this morning. They woke, the alarm went off at 10:00 so he sent the kids in to wake me up. Good thing I went out yesterday.

EXPERIMENTER: Why? What would he have done to you?

GEORGE: He'd yell, he'd yell and take it out on my mother, you know.

EXPERIMENTER: He would?

GEORGE: Yeah, he'd yell at her because I'm in, and then I went out after then. Why, I ain't seen my mother in two days . . . [unclear] yesterday morning. Stop looking at the bottom card.

EXPERIMENTER: I didn't look at anything. Don't give me a hard time now. I'm not cheating. You cheat, so you say I cheat and that covers up for your cheating.

GEORGE: No, it doesn't.

EXPERIMENTER: Yes, it does. You try to accuse everybody of what you do yourself.

GEORGE: Go ahead.

EXPERIMENTER: And in that way you think you're . . . How many cards you got?

GEORGE: Five, [unclear] five.

EXPERIMENTER: All right.
GEORGE: I'm not cheating. Go ahead. Go ahead.
EXPERIMENTER: You've got a card sitting in the donut box.
GEORGE: Yeah.
EXPERIMENTER: All right. Got it off the floor. [Boy laughs]
One or two?
GEORGE: One.
EXPERIMENTER: All right [laughs.]
GEORGE: One card and I'm out.

This card playing may have served some of the same functions as play therapy with younger children. Here the play was more sophisticated, however. Since the primary focus of attention of the boy is on the mechanics and outcome of the game, he does not feel threatened by the development of the positive relation with the experimenter. Also, he can avoid uncomfortable psychological interpretations made by the experimenter during the game by calling attention to some aspect of the game instead of responding to the experimenter. This situation also makes it possible for the boy to briefly interject important personal comments into the conversation if he wishes without the embarrassment of having to continue discussion about the comment.

Through this approach, the psychologist was able to establish close relations with the boys whom other agencies were unable to reach. Eventually, this card playing was alternated with standard interviews of an analytic type as described in the preceding section. The limitations and possibilities of this card-playing activity require further experimental evaluation.

It has been observed that delinquents in usual treatment programs often get into trouble with the law just before the termination of their therapy (Goldsmith, 1959). This may be an attempt on their part to continue the relationship—a way of saying to the therapist, "I still need you." Or, if the delinquent feels rejected and angry, his getting into trouble may be an attempt to hurt the therapist by saying, "See, you didn't really help me. I'm the same as I was before." Or it may be a combination of these factors.

The experimenters attempted to avoid these unfortunate results through a gradual termination procedure. As the job neared completion, the role relationship with the boy slowly changed from employer-employee to friend. After termination, the boy could stop by at the laboratory whenever he wanted just to talk or to have a coke. Sometimes the experimenter would meet the boy at a local cafeteria for dinner.

Immediately after termination, under these conditions, the boys would stop around the laboratory frequently, often three or four times a week. By the end of three months, however, the boys would stop by or phone perhaps only once every two weeks. From then on, the contacts gradually diminished until now, three years later, there is only an occasional phone call or letter. Occasionally an experimenter unexpectedly meets one of the boys on the street and they have coffee together. Or while the experimenter is driving through town, one of the boys may good-naturedly snowball the experimenter's car and then ask how things are going. The experimenters considered friendship an important experimental condition which might prevent a sudden increase in crime at the time of job termination. It was viewed as a part of the process of "weaning" the subject from his dependency on the experimenter.

Except in a few cases, termination from the laboratory job was planned to coincide with the boy's successful employment at another job. It was hoped that this other job would provide him with money and contacts for new friends. (Once a boy became accustomed to steady payment from the laboratory job, a full-time job outside the laboratory became quite attractive as he could easily earn two or three times more than he was earning at the laboratory.)

If a boy showed signs of getting into trouble with the police or having difficulties at work, the "weaning" process from the laboratory was slowed down and contact with the boy was increased. (Since the role of friend permits a wide variation in the number of meetings and the intensity of the relation, the experimenter could see a boy immediately when he called and arrange for additional meetings, if necessary.) If, on the other hand, things were going well, the experimenter might agree to see the boy the next day or talk to him later on the phone or arrange for a group of the boys to get together, instead of seeing the boy individually. In this way the length of time between meetings could be gradually increased and the intensity of the relation gradually decreased.

The data suggest a slight increase in the number of arrests during the first six months after the boys were terminated from the project as compared to the arrests during their employment at the laboratory. How this compares with the number of arrests which would have occurred if a more standard termination procedure had been used cannot be answered at this time. To the extent that clinical judgment is reliable, the experimenters felt that the termination procedure just described was moderately successful but still a far more difficult procedure than gaining the boys' attendance and cooperation.

Much of the experimenters' concern about termination centered around the fear that the friendships following termination would continue indefinitely. Obviously, the experimenters would not have time for all these friends nor would these friendships be at the level most meaningful for the experimenters. Being a friend to these boys could become a full-time job.

It is clear now that the friendships between the experimenters and subjects were not generally enduring. At the present time, even an occasional contact by phone or letter or accidental meeting holds true for less than one-quarter of the subjects. Friendships "faded" in the typical manner. This may be partially attributed to a geographical factor. Two of the experimenters have left the Boston area and one was away for a year. At least ten of the boys have spent time in the military service; five boys were incarcerated eight months or longer and several have moved out of the state.

There are some other factors which also may have lessened the possibility of enduring friendships. For example, the age difference between the experimenters and subjects makes subsequent association less likely. There are relatively few socially acceptable roles which encourage association between adult and adolescent males. Outside of such roles as "father," "priest," "coach," "teacher," "employer," and perhaps "therapist," "sponsor," or "friend of the family," association is often viewed with the suspicion of illicit social or sexual activity. The role relation of "friend" is not socially prominent. Some additional factors which may have hampered continued friendships are differences in vocational goals, educational level, marital status, preferred types of entertainment, and other conditions resulting from socioeconomic class differences.

In retrospect, termination went more smoothly than the

experimenters had at first expected. There were, of course, some quite difficult moments. One of the subjects, Ed, may serve as an illustration. Ed left the project to return to his home in a southern state. While there, he worked during the day and went to business school nights. Within two months he became dissatisfied and suddenly left home for a "vacation" in Boston. The boy's guardian in his home town (who had granted permission for Ed to participate in the project) immediately called the experimenter to warn him that Bill and a "parade" were on their way. A fifteen-year-old boy, wanted by the police, was with him. They were followed by his girl friend, sixteen, who was in turn followed by the girl's aunt, twenty-one, acting as the girl's "chaperone." (The chaperone had not notified her husband that she was leaving town.) The chaperone was in turn followed by detectives employed to find the fifteen-year-old boy.

The next day they all arrived on the experimenter's doorstep, literally, followed shortly by two detectives. The girl and her chaperone did not like the "tone" of the YWCA so with their own money they stayed at a Boston hotel. Within two days, room service had brought them $18.64 worth of shrimp cocktails.

Under the supervision of the chaperone and the experimenter, Ed and his girl were allowed to see each other. This supervision consisted of round-the-clock surveillance during which the girl was not allowed to leave the chaperone's sight nor Ed allowed to leave the experimenter's. After two days, the girl and her chaperone were getting tired from their exciting adventure and their money was almost gone. With happy memories of Boston, they left for home.

Meanwhile, the crime prevention bureau had picked up the fifteen-year-old boy and, with the help of the experimenter, contacted his anxious parents. The police informed the boy that if he rode back home on the bus by himself things would be straightened out at home by the time he arrived. They were, but not in his favor. When he arrived, he was arrested on violation of probation and sent to reform school. Ed was seen daily for the following week and a half and then three times a week for the next two weeks. He then returned home. He has subsequently married the girl and joined the Air Force. They are now living near an air base in a Northern state.

Another failure to terminate adequately is illustrated by the behavior of Dave. This boy attempted to follow the experimenter to Birmingham, Alabama, where the experimenter was moving. Instead of "following" the experimenter, however, Dave actually arrived in Birmingham ahead of the experimenter, who had stopped along the way to visit some relatives. He presented himself as a friend of the experimenter and was invited to stay in the home of one of the faculty members of the University of Alabama. There he lived as a "Southern gentleman" until the experimenter arrived. He later lived in the YMCA and worked briefly at the university. Unfortunately, Dave had never learned the manners of a Southern gentleman and so, for example, when he was introduced to someone he would just lower his head without replying. This behavior was seen by some of the white students as characteristic of a Negro. As his behavior became increasingly less tolerable, one student is reported to have commented, "There's nothing wrong with Dave—except his skin is the wrong color." Shortly after this, Dave moved on to look for new places in the South where he could be treated as a gentleman. He is now serving time in a Southern state prison for robbery. These incidents point out inadequacies in our termination procedure that need to be remedied in the future.

Part II: The Rationale

An Experimental View of Crime

The selection of an appropriate title for this section has presented considerable difficulty. The title above, while open to some misunderstanding, has been chosen to express my particular orientation. There are many theoretical orientations from which juvenile delinquency may be viewed. A person thinking about delinquency from a psychoanalytic orientation is likely to consider delinquency a form of mental illness, or a person thinking about delinquency from a sociological orientation is likely to consider delinquency the result of inadequate social opportunities. The task of this book is to present an experimental view of delinquency which considers delinquency a variety of behaviors that may be scientifically modified through experimental procedures. However, experimentation with human behavior cannot be intellectually or ethically removed from a careful consideration of the philosophical issues involved.

The answers that experimentation provides (for example, atomic energy) are not necessarily good, true, beautiful, or useful. They must be evaluated within a broader philosophical context of which experimentation and science are only a part. Experimental procedures are, after all, based upon a series of philosophical assumptions, and not even the most enthusiastic scientist will claim that the experimental method was handed down to man as a divine dictate. Science itself is open to revision, and even eventual elimination.

Furthermore, the decision as to which aspects of daily life are to be scientifically investigated involves many ethical issues. Consider, for example, the following incident.

In the fall of 1963, in Cambridge, Massachusetts, the body of the accused police-killer, Nicholas Yasaian, was found in the mud under a warehouse loading platform in a railroad freight yard. The twenty-two-year-old ex-convict died as a suicide victim from a lethal dose of sleeping pills. He had crawled under the warehouse during a rainstorm and lined the opening with papers and cardboard to keep out the wind and the rain. Three weeks earlier—before his robbery of a jewelry store and the subsequent shooting of a police-man—Nicholas was included in the last testament of a relative in Green Bay, Wisconsin. The surviving relatives had been unable to find him to inform him of the bequest. The boy's body, identified by his father, lay unclaimed in a funeral home.

The image of Nicholas as a worthless, poisoned animal crawling under a warehouse was far different from the image of him presented by the newspapers a few days earlier—the young, arrogant and brutal ex-convict. The effective, scientific prevention of murder, both of another person and of one's self, is not based upon shifting public opinion or even upon enduring public values. Scientific procedures are, ideally, based upon observations and con-clusions independent of ethical values. But the decision as to whether we should use a scientific procedure once we have developed it is an ethical and philosophical decision. Such a philosophical decision logically precedes the scientific, psy-chological question of what can be done to prevent such situations as the one in which Nicholas Yasaian was in-volved and died. (It should also be remembered that in the development of intellectual history, philosophy preceded psychology.) It is indeed surprising, then, that so many well organized delinquency programs fail to consider even briefly the philosophical rationale for their existence. It is perhaps for this reason that they often fail to design gen-uinely meaningful experiments.

Psychology, in its eagerness to establish itself as a discipline separate from philosophy, was almost "rebellious" in its claim to operate independently of ethical and moral issues. The evidence to the contrary, that therapists do indeed change their patients' ethical values in the direction of their own values, although reluctantly admitted by some therapists, is now quite clear (Murray, 1956; Frank, 1961; Reid, 1962). The patient seen by a Freudian analyst is very likely to acquire a Freudian view of the world; a client seen by a Rogerian counselor is likely to gain a Rogerian perspective (De Grazia, 1962). This commitment of therapists to particular ethical values may be illustrated by the goal of therapy as set forth by Harold Kelman, Dean of the American Institute of Psychoanalysis (1962, p. 124): "The main aim of future therapy may well be to promote wider and deeper here-now experiencing, guided by a theory of man which makes more possible the emergence of human spontaneity which is the charm of the child, the morality of a saint, the rigor of a scholar, the intuition of an artist and the maturity of a child-like adult." The moral imperatives here are clear, and the many philosophical issues which might be raised are apparent.

The theoretical orientation of our staff involves both an examination of the psychological processes of behavior change in an individual case and at the same time a consideration of the person's philosophical perspectives. In a sense, both process and content are simultaneously considered. We are finding it increasingly valuable to classify delinquents along a philosophical dimension as well as a psychological dimension. Some offenders might well be described along the philosophical dimension as primarily concerned about immediate physical pleasure (hedonism), or power over others (Chamberlain), or independence from social values (Nietzsche), or the absurdity of existence (nihilism). An example of an inmate who might easily be described in Nietzschian terms is a twenty-nine-year-old inmate whom I saw while he was incarcerated in a reformatory. He had previously been convicted of three armed robberies and numerous other offenses. His political shrewdness and hostility toward society were well known to prison authorities in several states. In this intellectually capable fellow hostility was combined with an intense, stylistic skill in writing.

As with the medieval serfs, does the same hold true today. With the most iron determination on our part and no shrinking back from anything, everyone amongst us must hold the view that we (the true philosophers) have been determined to fight the Christian religion to its very death—a life and death struggle. A long period of religion has not done us any good. With a manly bearing, we are the better men. On the opposite side, they are the weaker . . . In starting and waging campaigns it is not right that matters, but success. Close your hearts to pity! Act brutally! Two billion people must obtain what is their right. The stronger man is right. Be harsh and remorseless! Be steeled against all signs of compassion! Whoever has pondered over this world order knows that its meaning lies in the success of the best by means of force.

This sounds very much like two of his favorite writers, Nietzsche and Machiavelli. The approximately eighty philosophical discussions with him often involved, either implicitly or explicitly, a consideration of Nietzschian kindness and cruelty as well as the Nietzschian concept of "the genius of the heart."[1] Close attention was paid to psychological events such as transference, depression, insight as

[1] The genius of the heart, which imposes silence and attention on everything loud and self-conceited, which smooths rough souls and makes them taste a new longing—to lie placid as a mirror, that the deep heavens may be reflected in them;—the genius of the heart, which teaches the clumsy and too hasty hand to hesitate, and to grasp more delicately; which scents the hidden and forgotten treasure, the drop of goodness and sweet spirituality under thick dark ice, and is a divining-rod for every grain of gold, long buried and imprisoned in mud and sand; the genius of the heart, from contact with which everyone goes away richer; not

well as philosophical content. Before leaving the prison, but before a complete reconciliation between him and society could be effected, he wrote the following somber reflection on his life. A shift in orientation, an awareness of suffering is apparent.

Loneliness—complete and bitter loneliness—shattered ego, broken mirror of self "exposed." Where to now? Will I remain linked to this chain of self-destruction, this citadel of decay, this world of now worlds—or will I move amongst the living once again?

By being able to see with six eyes (senses) simultaneously, and with my sublime insight, for a few moments I saw the world as it really is, with all of its ugliness as well as its beauty, its destruction as well as its creation, wrong as well as right. Nature is so reckless in her design. So many wasted seeds to produce a single flower; so much needless suffering to round out a single life.

The usefulness of considering the philosophical orientation of offenders may also by illustrated, perhaps more adequately, by the case of a nineteen-year-old inmate. This boy, with a record of several auto thefts, nonsupport of his wife, and attempted suicide, was well mannered though somewhat sullen. In appearance, except for the prison uniform, he looked as though he belonged on the cover of a woman's magazine. With great reluctance, he agreed to be interviewed by a Streetcorner Research assistant. After four months of philosophically oriented interviewing, which centered largely around helping the boy think about his future, he casually brought in to the research assistant a paragraph he had written about a chest x-ray picture that had ap-

---

favoured or surprised, not as though gratified and oppressed by the good things of others; but richer in himself, newer than before, broken up, blown upon, and sounded by a thawing wind; more uncertain, perhaps, more delicate, more fragile, more bruised, but full of hopes which as yet lack names, full of a new will and current, full of a new ill-will and counter-current . . ." Friedrich Nietzsche, *The Philosophy of Nietzsche,* W. H. Wright, ed. (New York: Modern Library, 1954), pp. 608–609.

peared in the local newspapers. The picture showed the chest cavity of a woman who had swallowed a fork. The fork was brilliantly illumined against the dark, cloudy caverns of the woman's lungs. To his surprise, the assistant read the following:

The Golden Fork is finally being drawn upward, upward to eternal happiness. Upward out of the mysterious depths of the lost and unknown, and even the clutching fingers of death shall not prevent this journey to peace, joy, complete and everlasting happiness for it has found its place at long, long last after years of anguished, tormented searching . . . Finally, it has found the true path, the true way to this long-sought ecstasy, this contentment and peace beyond all explanation, this eternal happiness and beauty. So it cannot be stopped now, there is no power in the Universe to stop this rapturous flight to happiness, and it will make this journey, it must. It does make this journey successfully, remaining there forever, forever, a new and fully understood being.

After reading this, the assistant immediately called me out to the prison. Could this writing be a warning about another suicide attempt? Or, could this be a pre-schizophrenic escape into fantasy? My suggestion was to ask the boy. The boy was flattered by the interest in his writing because it was the only "serious" writing he had done except for letters to girl friends. To our surprise, the following story emerged.

He had, some time ago, fallen in "love" with another inmate, an inmate from whom he had received sincere respect and concern. This inmate had encouraged him, in moments of sadness, to look more deeply into the cause of that sadness. Following this advice, he began "doing research on my life while alone in the gym lifting weights." At our request, he described how the world finally became a "great place to live."

Who can say when I first discovered I was different from all these other beings (I was awfully young), it sprange up out of me suddenly, frighteningly, for all at once I realized I was all alone, by myself in this great, mysterious world of beings. I couldn't define exactly how I was different, but I realized in some way that I did not want physical objects, did not need them because I could never in my life be happy and contented with them alone. I began my tiresome, weary search seeking out another being, another companion who wanted what I wanted out of life, whose emotions and feelings were parallel with my own. I was given love from my family, yet I was not yet content with it for even they were not like me. They never really understood the real me, so I began to slip away from them, bottled up my feelings and emotions from them . . .

It dawned on me, the horrible suspicion was born that it was hopeless, that I could never, never in all my life find life itself. And I could not bear this terrible suspicion, knowing I could never be like the rest of you (ordinary people) for to me you were like death itself. I could never accept or even understand your cold physical way of life. So I tried desperately to take my own miserable life, to remove it forever from this cruel place, but even in that you interrupted me, prevented this escape from you . . .

I went on once again through life searching, probing into other lives for it, but still not finding it, until once again that tremendous depressing feeling was crushing me with a sense of hopelessness, until once again I was considering the merciful escape to death, but at long, long last this rapturous ecstasy, this thing of infinite beauty, this, oh I could never in all eternity explain my feelings, my emotions to you, to you I can only say I found this thing of beauty and wonder I was seeking, this being like myself with my own emotions and feelings—found myself. And at long, long last I am happy and content. All the beauties and tragedies of life have fallen open before me, I'm like a blind person come to life, gained my sight, found life itself . . . Yes, I searched and have finally been found.

> Tears of joy,
> Tears of love,
> I shed them freely, unashamedly,
> They flow at last, at long, long last.

It is now almost two years since this incident; the boy is married and employed as a mechanic. Somehow within this confused picture the formal diagnosis of manic-depressive neurosis seems incomplete without philosophical considerations. Surely the philosophical and ethical issues raised here are not easy. A clue, however, may be found in the striking resemblance of this boy's thoughts to the writings of the famous priest-paleontologist, Pierre Teilhard de Chardin, whose work this boy had never read or to his knowledge ever heard discussed. In his book, *The Divine Milieu* (1960), Teilhard de Chardin describes an "interior experiment" involving the examination of our most secret self leading "further and further away from the conventional certainties by which social life is superficially illuminated" and leading eventually to a joyous discovery called "my life," a part of the divine milieu.[2] A description of the arrival of the divine milieu for an individual is presented below. Note how growth is gradual but suddenly realized by the person; how the person searches but instead is finally drawn. These exact characteristics were described above by the inmate.

On some given day a man suddenly becomes conscious that he is alive to a particular perception of the divine spread every-

---

[2] An explanation of this experiment may be found on pages 48 to 49 of *The Divine Milieu* (New York: Harper & Row, 1960). Later, page 89, Teilhard de Chardin observes, "All around us, to right and left, in front and behind, above and below, we have only had to go a little beyond the frontier of sensible appearances in order to see the divine welling up and showing through. But it is not only close to us, in front of us, that the divine Presence has revealed itself. It has sprung up so universally, and we find ourselves so surrounded and transfixed by it, that there is no room left to fall down and adore it, even within ourselves. By means of all created things, without exception, the divine assails us, penetrates us and moulds us. We imagined it as distant and inaccessible, whereas in fact we live steeped in its burning layers. *In eo vivimus*. As Jacob said, awakening from his dream, the world, this palpable world, to which we brought the boredom and callousness reserved for profane places, is in truth a holy place, and we did not know it. *Venite, adoremus*."

where about him. Question him. When did this state begin for him? He cannot tell. All he knows is that a new spirit has crossed his life.

"It began with a particular and unique resonance which swelled each harmony, with a diffused radiance which haloed each beauty . . . All the elements of psychological life were in turn affected; sensations, feelings, thoughts. Day by day they became more fragrant, more coloured, more intense by means of an indefinable thing—the same thing. Then the vague note, and fragrance, and light began to define themselves. And then, contrary to all expectation and all probability, I began to feel what was ineffably common to all things. The unity communicated itself to me by giving me the gift of grasping it. I had in fact acquired a new sense, *the sense of a new quality or of a new dimension.* Deeper still: a transformation had taken place for me *in the very perception of being.* Thenceforward being had become, in some way, tangible and savorous to me; and as it came to dominate all the forms it assumed, being itself began to draw me and to intoxicate me."

This is what any man might say, more or less explicitly, who has gone any distance in the development of his capacity for self-analysis. Outwardly he could well be a pagan. (Teilhard de Chardin, 1960, pp. 108–109.)

These two cases of reformatory inmates have been presented with philosophical considerations merely to suggest that philosophical perspectives do not need to be eliminated from psychological experimentation and that they might even be useful in increasing psychological effectiveness. An experimental view of behavior does not necessarily regard delinquent behavior as a moral weakness, or a mental illness, or a response to stimuli. Nor does it exclude these interpretations. Perfectly acceptable experiments may be carried out, for example, using moral training with delinquents if three conditions are met. *First,* the results must be measured in terms of specific delinquent behaviors, not in terms of whether the delinquents are morally "better" afterwards. The statement that delinquents are "better" following a procedure is not a direct answer to the question of whether moral training can reduce the number of delinquent acts. Many programs that seek to develop better boys and girls leave the question of their genuine effectiveness in reducing crime essentially unanswered. It is often just assumed that such programs must be effective. *Second,* the situation and procedure used in the experiment should be clearly enough defined so that others can repeat the experiment. A study of the effect of prayer on the growth of plants (Leohr, 1959) is an example of an inadequately defined procedure. Prayer was not defined well enough to separate it from hope, extrasensory perception, concern, extra attention, and so forth. This same criticism of lack of definition applies to many techniques of psychotherapy— and certainly to some of the procedures used in this present study. Not every detail of a procedure or situation needs to be described, but critical variables need to be isolated and stated. *Third,* the situation, procedure, and techniques of measurement must be available to other investigators. If any of these involve critical variables that are not reproducible, then an experiment is not possible within the definition offered here. To the extent that psychoanalysis assumes that the *unique* interaction between patient and therapist is crucial to the outcome it is not an experimental procedure but rather a technical art.

An experimental view of behavior does not remove behavior-change programs from association with philosophy. Rather, it places the resultant behavioral and emotional modifications more directly in the context of philosophy than do even present programs of social work and mental health. Experimentation is based directly upon verification, and the criteria used for verification change as science changes its view of nature. Immediate answers, personal authority, and final solutions are questioned. Secondly, the psychological "experiment" comes closer to the early, exploratory work of Freud (in which the participants were called "subjects" instead of "patients") and to the questioning of philosophy than to the present therapeutic formalities of social work and psychoanalysis.[3] In his presidential address to the American Psychiatric Association, Kenneth Appel (1954, p. 8) commented: "Plato and the Socratic dialogues have given me great help in my professional work: the searching quest, the lack of dogmatism, the importance of tolerance, recognition of other people's points of view, and interest in others." Therapists cannot escape the espousal of human values such as knowing oneself or the courage to explore reality; nor can they escape this responsibility for acquiring technological skills commensurate with their responsibility. They are thus, perhaps unwittingly, both philosophers and scientists. The participants in the therapeutic experiment, whether called doctors and patients or experimenters and subjects, may thus proceed "inspired by love and guided by knowledge" toward that excellent life so fervently advocated by Spinoza long ago.

[3] Freud's early treatment of hysteria involved a series of experimental procedures including rest, massage, hydrotherapy, electrical stimulation, hypnotic catharsis, and finally, in 1893, psychoanalysis. In 1893, Freud wrote, "Information may also be found . . . concerning the toilsome but completely reliable method of psychoanalysis which I use in making these investigations and by which at the same time the investigations serve a therapeutic purpose." See Sigmund Freud, *Collected Papers*, ed. Ernest Jones (New York: Basic Books, 1959), p. 115.

Within the limitations of experimentation cited above, the content of an experiment depends largely on the interests of the experimenter. The experimenters in the Streetcorner Research project used an approach in designing experiments which involves a sequence of four analytical steps. This analysis is particularly useful in suggesting methods for bringing about new behavior. Textbooks rarely deal precisely with techniques for producing new behavior, which is often assumed to arise "spontaneously," "from within the individual," "as a result of environmental changes," or by "working through previous problems." These explanations are experimentally unsatisfactory.

Behavioral analysis as used by the experimenters involved a four-step sequence: 1) Defining the final, desired behavior as specifically as possible in measurable units. 2) Determining the subject's repertoire of present and previous behavior. 3) Determining the available reinforcers (negative or positive) which are most likely to be effective. 4) Applying the reinforcers according to an explicit theoretical model and modifying application according to results (feedback).

These four steps may be illustrated briefly by their application to the problem of getting a group of delinquents to take movies of their gang activity. This would be new behavior for these delinquents. The specific behavior desired would be the filming of the gang's spontaneous daily life activity at three- to five-day intervals with an 8 mm electric-eye camera. The accomplishment of this behavior would be measured by the number of feet of processed film turned over to the experimenter by the gang. As far as the experimenter could determine, none of the boys in this lower-working-class gang had previously run a movie camera, ever met the experimenter, or heard about the Streetcorner Research project. (This experiment was conducted in a city twenty miles distant from the other work of the project.) The reinforcers available and immediately useable were money, gang and community prestige, feelings of accomplishment, and excitement (intrigue). The actual application of these reinforcers occurred in the following manner as indicated by the experimenter's notebook.

Several days prior to the experimenter's entry into the gang's territory, he obtained the name of the leader, Bongo. On Sunday, November 13, 1960, the experimenter drove around the gang's section of the city from 5 P.M. until 7:30 P.M. His driving around aroused the curiosity of the boys hanging around the corners and in the doorways. Occasionally he stopped for coffee at a restaurant or diner. Shortly after 7:30 he stopped just outside the gang's territory and asked a rival gang where he could find Bongo. They said that Bongo usually hung out at a warehouse across from Jimmy's Market. The experimenter had deliberately asked the wrong group for Bongo so that rumors would get back to Bongo's gang that someone was looking for him. The experimenter then left town and did not return for two days.

On the following Wednesday, between 9:00 and 9:15 in the evening, the experimenter stopped his car in front of the warehouse. Several boys were standing there, but not Bongo. When he asked for Bongo, none of the boys moved from the doorway or answered. The experimenter explained that he was looking for Bongo to give him a job. The job would be taking movies. "I'm on the level, and here's the camera." The gang was noticeably impressed by the new, streamlined camera. A spokesman for the gang stepped forward a few steps, "What's the movies for?" The experimenter explained that he worked for an outfit that wanted films of what a gang's daily life is like because some people who live in fancy places wouldn't believe it unless they saw films of it. "The job works like this. Bongo rents the camera for fifty cents a week and he buys film from us cheap. Then he takes the pictures and sends the film away to get it developed. The company that develops it, sends it directly back to Bongo. When Bongo gets it, we all look it over. If the outfit likes the film, they'll buy it at fifty cents a minute. What they don't want they don't have to buy. And, Bongo doesn't need to sell them any film if he doesn't want to. He's in charge of the film." By this time the boys were up to the car listening. The experimenter again asked where he could find Bongo, and the spokesman replied that he usually showed up at the corner at 10:00. The experimenter then offered to pay the spokesman one dollar if Bongo was waiting on the corner at 10:00 whether or not he decided to take the job. When the experimenter arrived shortly after 10:00, three boys, including Bongo, were standing on the curb. The spokesman pointed to Bongo and was immediately handed a dollar by the experimenter. Bongo said nothing so the experimenter again explained the job. Bongo then asked, "How come you picked me?" The experimenter replied, "You're pretty important around this place, and seem like a clever guy. We need someone who's sort of 'with it' to do this job because it hasn't been done before. If you do a good job, you get a couple dollars in your pocket every week. If you do a bad job, nothing."

When Bongo asked when he could start, he was told not to make up his mind now but to think it over. (This is a reversal of usual "con" procedures in which the operator tries to get the person to make a decision as soon as possible.) He and the experimenter set a meeting time in the afternoon of the next day. Bongo was shown how to run the camera and within four days he, several friends, and the experimenter viewed the first film. During the following eight weeks the amount of film produced each week varied widely from twenty feet per week to seventy-five feet. After this the amount of film produced each week began to level out to forty to sixty feet per week. The films typically contained shots of friends standing on streetcorners, kids playing in the railroad yard, girls walking along the street, cars, card games, family scenes, and so forth. A gradual change in the content and style of the films was noticed over several months at the same time that the experimenter observed a change in the behavior of the gang, but this has not been studied systematically.

Another example of the application of behavioral analysis to a specific problem is the procedure used to gain the delinquents' attendance at the laboratory. This procedure has been previously described in the section on gaining delinquent attendance and cooperation. In both cases, the new behavior was initially quite variable in its occurrence and then gradually became regular as it was brought under stimulus control. The acquisition and maintenance of new behaviors require the careful use of positive and negative reinforcers. The use of a reinforcer, such as giving a bonus for a job well done, is an incident which may produce considerable emotion in the person receiving it. The fact that such a reward may be given according to certain rules (as in a contest) or according to a certain fixed or variable schedule does not necessarily reduce its personal meaning or impact. Consider, for example, the frequent trips a person is likely to make to his mailbox when waiting for a very important package. The fact that the person's increased trips to the mailbox may be accurately predicted or that he can be expected to open rapidly the awaited package before the other mail does not reduce the person's pleasure in receiving the package. Words such as "stimulus control," "response," or "schedules of reinforcement" may sound cold and impersonal when used to describe and predict behavior, but so do the words "plasma protein," "hematemesis," or "radioactive sodium chromate technic" when applied to the diagnosis of a duodenal ulcer. The patient's pain is real and the alleviation of that pain depends upon the doctor's understanding and use of such words. The emotional connotation of these words should not be confused with the situational, experiential reality to which they refer. The familiar saying, "a map is not the territory," applies here. Furthermore, if it should become popularly known that the most effective schedules for the production of human behavior involve reinforcers such as love, mutual respect, sexual satisfaction, accomplishment, religious experience, or the kindly surprise, the language of behavioral technology might well become the language of poets in subsequent generations.

Increasingly, schedules of reinforcement and related procedures are being applied to important human problems. It is possible to develop through the use of reinforcement procedures cooperation between young children (Azran and Lindsley, 1956). Or, alternatively, it is possible, through the use of moving pictures showing aggressive role models, to increase the aggressive behavior of children (Bandura, Ross, and Ross, 1961). It is also possible to teach very young children to read (Staats, Minke, Finley, Wolf, and Brooks, 1962; Fowler, 1962). With adults, through the arousal of needs, and the design of means of satisfying these needs, conformity to group pressure can often be obtained (Walker and Heyns, 1962). Finally, many standard clinical symptoms of "mental illness" have been experimentally treated with encouraging results and with much less expenditure of professional time than that required by the more traditional methods.[4]

[4] Some of these symptoms have been: enuresis (Martin and Kubly, 1955), stammering (Cherry and Sayers, 1954), phobias (Friedman, 1950; Lang and Lazovik, 1963), homosexuality (Salter, 1949; Blakemore, Thorpe, Barker, Conway, and Lavin, 1963), neuroses (Herzberg, 1945; Wolpe, 1962; Lazarus, 1963) and schizophrenia (King, Armitage, and Tilton, 1958; Peters and Jenkins, 1954; Ayllon, 1963).

The delinquent and nondelinquent worlds most often clash in moments of impulse and violence, and these are moments of intense experience for both the delinquent and the victim. The solution of delinquency problems may require the same sharp impact. That is, the nondelinquent culture may have to reach the delinquent culture through scientific strategies which include the dimension of intensity. A typical example of dramatic impact is that of a social worker who walks completely unknown into the home of a delinquent and by his confidence and enthusiasm radically changes the life of the delinquent. Such a procedure, however, frequently overlooks the use of scientific strategy. Psychological experimentation is now providing an increasing number of scientific techniques for modifying behavior, which may be of much benefit. The nondelinquent world is made up of philosophers, scientists, professors, businessmen, government officials, and millions of capable, respectable citizens. It would indeed be a sad commentary if this nondelinquent population, tremendously outweighing delinquents in mental, political, and financial resources, could not, at least, "outwit" the delinquent or, at most, gain his enthusiastic participation in socially productive activities. Yet, this is apparently the case. A new strategy is required.

Let us briefly examine two cases of the use of strategy, or behavioral technology, in the reduction of auto theft. In an east coast industrial town, with a population of approximately one hundred thousand, auto thefts by juveniles suddenly increased to such an extent that public announcements were made over the radio reminding car owners to lock their cars. These radio announcements and the increased arrests of juveniles did not solve the problem. As nearly as could be determined, the majority of the thefts were committed by two gangs. The cars were not damaged, sold, or even, apparently, used for temporary transportation. The auto thefts seemed to be a means of achieving gang prestige. If a gang member was caught and sent to reform school, this increased the "high-risk value" of the activity and, thus, it became even more attractive to the gang. On the other hand, if a gang member was caught and given a suspended sentence, his status in the gang increased because he had "conned" the judge. Neither the usual "getting-tough" approach or the "being-soft" approach worked.

During an informal discussion of the problem among city officials, a judge, and a court chaplain, the chaplain suggested that the boys be fined for stealing cars since this would have a negative meaning for them. There is, however, no law in the state that permits fining juveniles for stealing. The judge, who liked the idea, suggested an alternative. There is a state law that permits fining drivers who are not adequately insured. Why not fine the boys for driving without adequate insurance? A few days later a gang member appeared in court charged with the illegal use of a motor vehicle and with driving without adequate insurance. He was found guilty of both charges, given a suspended sentence, and ordered to report to his probation officer each week to pay a fifty-dollar fine. The boy dejectedly left the courtroom almost in tears. There were several similar court cases during the next few weeks. The number of auto thefts then decreased markedly and remained at its usual low rate. The problem of gang auto thefts was apparently solved.

The second case that illustrates the use of strategy in reducing auto theft concerns the thefts committed by the boys in the Streetcorner Research project. Here, a different sequence of behavior was operative in producing auto thefts. Interviews with the boys indicated that they "stole cars to be used as temporary transportation to get to a specific location or just to drive around." After they had used the car, they abandoned it. Further investigation showed that they could not borrow their friends' cars because they had no driver's licenses. They did not have licenses because they were afraid of failing, or had actually failed, the written part of the license examination. The boys were then helped by the Streetcorner Research project to read and understand the *Driver's Handbook*. (The procedure used to teach these boys has been described in an earlier section.) After they acquired licenses, the number of auto thefts committed by this group greatly decreased.

The design of the strategy used in each of these situations involved first the functional analysis of the behavioral sequence before, during, and after the theft of the car. The strategy then involved the breaking of this behavioral sequence at the most feasible point, as judged by our knowledge of community structure and behavioral science. One could, of course, eliminate auto theft by eliminating cars. Or, one could give cars to delinquents who have records of stealing them (which might be less expensive than spending $3500 per year to keep a boy in reform school), but this would probably promote auto theft by others. Intervention which is focused upon a particular behavior such as auto theft must also consider the broader aspects of community organization and aftereffects.

The mere application of the strategy used in the first case would most probably have been ineffective if used in the second situation. It is important, therefore, not to imitate strategies but to develop them in response to the specific realities of a particular situation. Because the behavioral scientist's knowledge of the social aspects of a problem in a given community may be limited, he can often use to a great advantage two types of consultants: 1) community leaders who are thoroughly familiar with the social structure, and 2) people who create or "have" the problem which is to be solved. If delinquency is to be reduced in a given area, the delinquents living in that area are the "experts" on that crime. They may be hired as experimental subjects, research assistants, or consultants to provide valuable information that would not be obtainable in any other way.

An effectively designed strategy has impact upon the target population, and, conversely, impact may be considered a form of strategy. Thus, although strategy and impact may be discussed separately, they probably occur simultaneously in effective programs (in the same way that the height and width of a table may be discussed independently yet both must be present for the table to actually exist). The fact that behavioral science focuses on changing behavior does not exclude personal experience from consideration. The production of new personal experiences may be considered one of the most effective techniques for the production of new behaviors. We not only experience ourselves into ways of behaving but behave ourselves into ways of experiencing (Bruner, 1962).

Equipped with the ability to develop a strategy, create an impact, and scientifically evaluate the result, the experimenter may enter directly into the delinquent subculture expecting to produce significant behavior change. It is at this level of the actual social contact among individuals of the delinquent and nondelinquent cultures that many programs seem to most seriously fail. Moral injunctions and exhortation are not adequate; and legal punishment, beyond that necessary social protection for behaviors which neither the individual nor society can change, may be considered a form of ineffective cruelty. Longer sentences do not permanently reduce subsequent crime (Frym, 1956). The alternative is the design of a humane technology which will eliminate unwanted behaviors and develop in their place desirable behaviors. How, for example, shall society implement the ancient moral injunctive, "Love thy neighbor"? Here observations of Aldous Huxley (1961, pp. 71–72) are appropriate:

How can we increase the amount of love in the world? How can we elicit from individuals their potentialities for friendliness and for love, and how can we, if possible, do something constructive about their potentialities for violence and aggression? Here again we find another strange factor. Whereas all the great religions have insisted upon the importance of love— Christian charity or Buddhist universal compassion—very little has been done in the way of suggesting means whereby love can be actualized on a wider scale and in a deeper way. It is a strangely ironical fact that, as far as I know, the only people who have gone out deliberately to create in their children a prejudice in favor of friendliness are an extremely small and primitive tribe described by Margaret Mead in New Guinea, the Arapesh. These people have used the best possible Pavlovian method for creating prejudice in favor of universal love. The mother as she nurses her child strokes the child so the child is enjoying both the pleasure of eating and the pleasure of being stroked and being in contact with the mother, and while this is happening the mother will rub the child against other members of the family or against anybody who happens to be around, or even against the domestic animals which roam about the huts, and murmur, "Good, good." The child, of course, does not understand the word at that time, but it certainly understands the tone of voice; and as soon as it learns to speak it knows what the meaning of the word "good" is and therefore associates this extremely pleasurable experience of being fed and of being caressed with being brought into intimate contact with other human beings and with animals. According to Margaret Mead, this method is immensely effective.

These people are exceedingly friendly, and it is, as I say, a curiously ironic thing that it has remained for this primitive people in the remote area of New Guinea to have invented an effective way of creating a prejudice in favor of friendliness.

In a less dramatic manner, reinforcement procedures have been experimentally used to produce cooperation between children. Azran and Lindsley (1963) had twenty children, seven to twelve years of age, form into ten teams of two each. If the children cooperated in getting a light to go on, jelly beans fell into a cup sitting on the table between them. If they did not cooperate, the light would not go on and no jelly beans would fall into the cup. The children were not told that they could cooperate. All the teams learned to cooperate within the first ten minutes of experimentation, and leader-follower patterns were characteristic. When reinforcement was discontinued, co-operative responses significantly decreased. This simple straightforward experiment points the way toward designing effective social-change techniques. Mere injunction, or kindness, and even the best intentions of streetcorner workers will not alone be maximally effective in reducing adolescent crime. A humane technology, strategically applied, is required.

Some Considerations Governing Experimentation with Social Problems

Even more serious than the present lack of techniques for changing behavior is the absence of a philosophical context in which new techniques may be experimentally developed and utilized. Often when evidence is presented to the public that behavior and experience can be effectively changed by the use of specific techniques, the public and even some researchers are not certain that they want additional techniques developed. Although there is little public objection to behavior-change "psychotherapeutic" techniques used with frankly psychotic or neurotic patients, there is no reason to believe that such techniques will be always confined to such limited populations. Further, many significant behavior-change techniques may be developed in psychological laboratories with normal subjects and these techniques may be directly available for use with the general public. An example is the development of subliminal advertising which, even though evidence was not entirely clear as to its effectiveness (Schwitzgebel, 1958), resulted in a generally negative public reaction with very little support for research into the ways in which subliminal stimulation might be constructively used. Effective techniques may be socially dangerous as well as socially beneficial. The necessary social structure for the constructive use of behavioral technology—as an important alternative to the destructive use of this technology or the suppression of scientific inquiry—is not yet well established.

Fundamental to the development of behavior-change techniques and their socially constructive use is a willingness to discover and acknowledge behavior as it actually exists in day-to-day living.

Geologists, biologists, chemists, and physicists know in considerable detail about the distribution in nature of the materials and processes with which they deal . . .

In contrast, psychologists know little more than laymen about the frequency and degree of occurrence of their basic phenomena in the lives of men—of deprivation, of hostility, of freedom, of friendliness, of social pressure, of rewards and punishments. Although we have daily records of the behavior of volcanoes, of the tides, of sun spots, and of rats and monkeys, there have been few scientific records of how a human mother cared for her young, how a particular teacher behaved in the classroom and how the children responded, what a family actually did and said during a mealtime, or how any boy lived his life from the time he awoke in the morning until he went to sleep at night. Because we lack such records, we can only speculate on many important questions . . .

Moreover, the lack of field data limits the discovery of some of the laws of behavior. It is often impossible to create in the laboratory the frequency, the duration, the scope, the complexity, and the magnitude of some conditions that it is important to investigate. In this, psychology has much in common with meteorology. Some of the principles of the whirlwind and the thunderbolt can be studied in the laboratory, but to extend the curves into the high values, and to include all complicating factors, it is necessary to go to the plains and to observe these events as they occur under natural conditions. In principle, the same is true in psychology for studies of conditions which are frequent in daily life, but which are difficult to create experimentally. This should not be discouraging. Experiments in nature are occurring every day. We need only the techniques and facilities to take advantage of them. (Barker and Wright, 1954, pp. 2–3.)

The reluctance of the public to acknowledge the Kinsey Reports and their subsequent widespread effects (Geddes, 1954) indicate the problem of public denial which social research faces. It is difficult to conduct significant research on social problems, and even more difficult to gain public understanding of that research if the public does not honestly look at the behavior which is to be changed. Certainly a part of the difficulty lies in the great difference between the standards of "proper" behavior established by law and custom and the actual, covert behavior of many "proper" people. We may see this situation perhaps more clearly by looking back to eighteenth-century France where the difference between public standards and actual behavior in the area of sex was probably greater than even in our present culture. Sadistic sexual practices were strictly forbidden yet they were so frequent that sadistic pornography was sold almost openly and the torture of criminals in public squares provided almost daily entertainment.

Diaries and legal papers indicate that someone was hanged or broken on the wheel nearly every other day in the public squares of Paris, and occasionally someone was burned alive or torn apart by horses. Now and then it might take a day or two for a hardy wretch to die dangling on the wheel, and it was far from uncommon for him to scream for water throughout the first night. The torturing and quartering of Damiens, the would-have-been assassin of Louis XV, took an especially long time, since he was stronger than the four horses assigned to pull him apart. In the end the public executioner had to help the horses by hacking the victim's muscles with an axe. Vantage points were sold all about the square for that event and hawkers of balloons roamed through the crowd. Casanova was one of the onlookers, but he actually did most of his looking at two women on the balcony near him . . . (Taylor, 1963, p. 199.)

This situation is shocking in part because of the great discrepancy between the values publicly proclaimed and the actual daily behavior of most people. The reluctance of the public to honestly acknowledge undesirable behavior patterns has contributed to a severe scarcity of factual data about the daily-life behavior of even normal people. The painful honesty which is required of mental patients is also now required of the general public if it genuinely desires the alleviation of its social problems.

Because many social problems cannot be studied in isolation in the laboratory, experiments dealing with these problems must be conducted within the community (Schwitzgebel, 1961; Schwitzgebel and Kolb, 1964). For example, it has been informally observed by McClelland at Harvard (1951) that the traditional laboratory measures on tea, coffee, and alcohol cannot account for their widespread usage in our society. Hence, even the study of a phenomenon as common as the use of these beverages must move beyond the confines of the usual experimental laboratory. There are also other phenomena such as love, anger, and religious experience which cannot very well be brought into the laboratory in their genuine form. These may be studied in their natural setting.[5] Ideally, research on social problems should be done directly on the change process where it occurs in the community (Chein, Cook, and Harding, 1948). Thus, experimentation is gradually moving into the community (Schwitzgebel, 1963b).

Experimental programs within the community must have clear criteria for measuring the success or failure of various activities and results should be frequently evaluated. If an activity succeeds it deserves continued support, if it fails it should be discontinued. Social experiments cannot guarantee positive results from all their activities, otherwise they would not be experiments. This, as Kubie (1961) has noted, requires courage:

[5] Fine (1960) has suggested: "Historically, such a search for [general] laws derived from [psychology] experiments stems from an incorrect analogy. The laboratory situations upon which physics, chemistry and other sciences depend are exactly analogous to real life; no extrapolation is necessary. At most there is a difference in size or complexity." Additional discussion may be found in Shoben (1961), Skinner (1959, pp. 223–241), McClelland (1951), and Shands (1960, pp. 199–203).

Those who represent the world of the mind and of the spirit must acquire the humility which led medicine to study its defeats at the autopsy table. This was a unique moment in human culture. We need now to apply the same self-scrutiny to all of culture. And as we do this, let us stop to remind ourselves that when a patient dies, the doctor does not blame the patient; he blames himself. But when humanity fails, the artists and the writers scold, and the theologian thunders angry denunciations of human deficiencies, when they should be turning a pitiless scrutiny on themselves, their beliefs, and their techniques. My challenge is to the courage and dignity of doubting, and to the duty of testing and experimenting.

Personnel in experimental programs should feel free enough within the structure of adequate safeguards and supervision to try new, inventive techniques. A social experiment does not promise success. It does, however, promise sincere effort, new techniques, and a scientific evaluation of results. The freedom to make mistakes of limited consequence is a prerequisite for inventive social programs.

The experimental methods used in communities will necessarily seem simple, and even foolish, in comparison to the complexity of the situations in which they will be applied. Perhaps experimentation will, in fact, turn out to be impossible in natural settings until more refined methods are developed for the measurement and control of many variables simultaneously. On the other hand, simplicity may turn out to be an advantage. Morison has noted that medicine's success in controlling infectious diseases has occurred through the use of rather simple ideas of causality which usually selected as "The Cause" that element in the situation which one could do the most about. He has also observed that, "There is a general impression, presumably quite true, that delinquency is the result of a number of complex factors . . . Even if we could describe them, it is not obvious that such a description would help much in solving the problem" (1960, p. 194). Experimentation aimed directly at the reduction of crime will have to work with variables which can be altered within the present social situation. Judge David Bazelon (1961), United States Court of Appeals for the District of Columbia, has commented that many critics "fear the unknown contours of a future dominated by the experimental ideas of rehabilitation. Reformers may share some of these fears, but they are motivated even more by the fear of the consequences of continuing our present practices." Shannon (1961), a sociologist, has pointed out the need for research and experimentation within the delinquent's natural habitat.[6]

The increasing use of experimentation to find solutions to significant daily problems such as delinquency is raising new ethical issues. As long as experimentation was confined to the study of nonsense syllables, ethics were not very difficult. Volunteers could come to the laboratory and enjoy (or heroically endure) science. However, now that experimentation is moving into more common life situations, the ethical issues are much greater. Will this experimentation lead people into viewing themselves as mere objects of study (Seeley, 1960), or to a fractionation of sensibility (Kahler, 1957), or to neglecting our humanness (Rogers, 1961), or to a tyranny over the mind (Huxley, 1958)? Or will experimentation lead instead to the mature survival of mankind (Skinner, 1956), the realization of inner potentialities (May, 1958), and man's discovery of the "deep center of the timeless moment" (Martin, 1960)? The answer is not clear. But scientific experimentation with vital human behavior has begun and there is no turning back.

---

[6] Some programs which have moved in this direction are the Cambridge-Somerville Youth Study (McCord, McCord, and Zola, 1959), the Hyde Park Youth Project (Grandy, 1959), the Boston Delinquency Project (Miller, 1957), the Chicago Area Project (Kobrin, 1959), and the New York City Youth Board projects (New York City Youth Board, 1956).

A science of human behavior which is not utilized by persons with a deep moral regard for human experience will be utilized by persons without such regard. Ethics of use should evolve with the discovery of possible application. Skinner (1959, p. 11) has commented:

> Science has turned up dangerous processes and materials before. To use the facts and techniques of a science of man to the fullest extent without making some monstrous mistake will be difficult and obviously perilous. It is no time for self-deception, emotional indulgence, or the assumption of attitudes which are no longer useful. Man is facing a difficult test. He must keep his head now, or he must start again—a long way back.

Not only must the results of experimentation be ethically considered, but the process of experimentation itself must be examined. We still painfully remember the terrible "experimentations" of the Nazis, and many illegitimate pregnancies have resulted from "just experimenting a little." The American Medical Association (1946, p. 1090) has set forth three principles regarding experimental research:

1) The voluntary consent of the person on whom the experiment is to be performed.
2) The danger of each experiment must be previously investigated by animal experimentation.
3) The experiment must be performed under proper medical protection and management.

The "Code Governing the Use of Students as Subjects in Research" issued by the Department of Social Relations, Harvard University (1960) is much more relevant to experimentation on mental processes and behavior. It affirms that "the relationship between investigator and subject must always be viewed in the larger context of the ethics of human relations in general" and that "in all dealings with students its [the department's] primary concern is for their instruction and welfare." It then lists eight principles in particular:

1) The experimental project shall not expose the student to undue risk to physical health or mental well-being.

2) All persons involved in initiating, approving, or conducting an experimental project shall be aware of a joint responsibility for the welfare of the students participating.

3) Student participation shall be voluntary, and pressure shall not be used to bring students to participate unwillingly.

4) Whenever possible the experimental project shall contribute positively to the student's educational experience in college.

5) The student shall be given a full and candid account of the purpose of the experiment. If it is impracticable to do so at the outset, he shall receive as soon as it is practicable a correct explanation of the experiment in which he has participated.

6) Care shall be taken that the student's time is not invaded to the extent of creating serious conflict with his other college duties.

7) Any experiment involving physical change (e.g., the use of drugs or alterations of diet) shall be approved in advance by proper authority in the University Health Services.

8) Any instructor who supervises experiments conducted by graduate or undergraduate students shall be responsible for seeing that these rules are strictly observed.

This code, one of the more adequate ones, is very much in keeping with the ten points of the Nuremberg Code (Nuremburg Military Tribunals, 1947), which is becoming a general standard for the West and has been adopted by the United States Public Health Service. Although the general objectives of these codes can be readily agreed with, actual practice raises many perplexing issues. A few examples of these issues will be presented here to indicate the complexity of the practical situation.

The Harvard University code states that participation shall be voluntary (point 3) and that the student shall be given an account of the purpose of the experiment at the outset unless it is impracticable, in which case he shall receive a correct explanation as soon as practicable (point 5). But in the case of an experiment involving a placebo, how can the experimenter know that the subject approves of a placebo being used—particularly if the placebo proves to be ineffective with the subject? Sometimes the information which must be withheld to conduct some experiments may be the very information which would change the subject's mind about volunteering.

Can experimentation be conducted only with those who expressly volunteer? Must prisoners, therefore, approve experimental programs in probation? What would be done with patients in a mental hospital who refused to participate in an experiment which involved developing the hospital into a therapeutic community? What consent is necessary from persons involved in community welfare and educational experiments?

There is certainly common agreement that the student should not be exposed to undue risk to physical health or mental well-being (point 1). But how is risk to be determined in certain initial experiments, and what may be considered "undue"? Does the phrase "mental health or mental well-being" include financial, moral, social, and political risk? And what are the limits of risk for the experimenter himself while working in areas having a high incidence of infectious diseases, or while dealing with aggressive behavior, or while doing necessary and perfectly ethical experimentation not yet legally sanctioned?[7]

Western society has not yet clearly defined the role of experimentation. As investigators move their research out

[7] Additional discussion of these issues may be found in Shimkin (1953), Guttentag (1953), Lasagna and von Felsinger (1953), and Mitscherlick (1949). Ladimer (1957) has outlined some of the legal aspects of experimentation, and Ivy (1948) has presented an historical view of the development of ethics in experimentation.

of the laboratory into natural settings, the possibilities of significant discovery increase, but so do the theoretical and ethical complexities. "On top of all his other problems, the harassed investigator recognizes . . . that sometimes to prevent an experiment may of itself be also an experiment, even a dangerous one!" (Beecher, 1958, p. 36.) The future of experimentation in society is not clear, nor is the future of society without experimentation on important issues. Perhaps the best situation is that in which experimentation is used within a context of broad social and philosophical perspectives toward humane goals.

It took me a long time to see how the path through literature and history and the path through evolutionary science and the experimental laboratory could converge honestly and without giving up their specific messages, could converge at points of new vistas, new outlooks, for the study of man . . . We are proud of the new vistas of today, but sure that they are not final; sure that other men are tramping on paths as rich and promising as our own and destined to converge upon us higher up. (Murphy, 1961, p. 114.)

If the strategy for reducing the frequency of a delinquent act is simply the imposition of a fine, as it was in the case cited above of car thefts by juvenile gangs, personality seems to be an unimportant factor. If, however, the change in delinquent behavior is to be the result of some change in the personality of the delinquent as through interviewing, then the personality of the experimenter may be of critical importance. The significance of the personality of the therapist has been suggested by many authors.[8] A positive relation between the patient and therapist tends to produce greater therapeutic results than a relationship which is not positive (Parloff, 1961; Wilson, 1960). In one of Freud's first publications on psychotherapy he commented, "I cannot imagine bringing myself to delve into the psychical mechanism of a hysteria in anyone who struck me as low-minded and repellent, and who, on closer acquaintance, would not be capable of arousing human sympathy."[9] Reports directly from Freud's patients indicate that his method was often warm and informal (Wortis, 1954; *The Wolf Man*, 1958; Doolittle, 1956). Others, such as Rogers (1957) discuss "unconditional positive regard" as being essential. Halpern and Lesser (1960) discuss the need for empathy, Mullan and Sangiuliano (1960) the need for "affective honesty" and Weigert (1960, p. 131) "the need

[8] For example, Betz and Whitehorn (1956), Strupp (1958), Parloff (1956), Arbuckle (1960), Alexander (1958), Fiedler (1953), Fenichel (1954, ch. 18), June (1953, pp. 71–96), Devereux and Hoffman (1961), West and Rafferty (1958).

[9] Cited by J. D. Frank, from Freud's "Studies on Hysteria," in *Persuasion and Healing* (Baltimore: Johns Hopkins Press, 1961), p. 130.

. . . for the creative process of mutual understanding which redeems the individual from the rigidities of defense and the anguish of loneliness." Frank (1961, p. 130) has summarized the situation: "It is generally agreed that the success of a psychotherapist depends in part on his really caring about the patient's welfare."

For the purposes of study, we would like to classify therapists and experimenters as "orthodox" or "unorthodox." This is not to suggest at all that orthodoxy regarding behavioral norms is a unitary trait. Rather, we want to investigate the possibility that there are certain personality characteristics that occur under the vague heading of unorthodoxy which do not occur under the heading of orthodoxy, and then determine whether these characteristics are useful in reducing juvenile crime. The terms orthodox and unorthodox are only meant to point the way toward these still unspecified characteristics. Tappan (1960, p. 527) has straightforwardly suggested that "relatively unorthodox methods of casework are fundamental to preventive and correctional treatment." Josselyn (1957, p. 16) has observed that ". . . often the most successful therapeutic results with this age group [adolescents] either are attained inexplicably, by seemingly unorthodox therapy, or by means scarcely justifying the dignity inherent in the concept of psychotherapeutic methods . . ."

Melitta Schmideberg, an analyst widely recognized in her treatment of major criminals, deliberately uses an unprofessional manner, may stand bail for her patients, introduces them to colleagues, and so forth (Schmideberg, 1955, pp. 188–189). Strean cites the following unorthodox therapeutic procedures by Anna Freud:

Bob, age 14, a thin, emaciated, easily intimidated youth, extremely withdrawn and asocial, fatherless and friendless, saw the therapist as a God. Despite the transcendental powers of the therapist, in the treatment situation Bob was a bigger God and mocked the therapist at every opportunity. "I know you think you are a big shot, you makes lots of dough and read guys' minds but I got your number. I can see through you better than you can see through me." As treatment went on Bob brought in tall stories of his journeys to planets and outer space where he "licked superman tooth and nail." However, the therapist always responded triumphantly that he had been to these planets many times and in fact had trained Superman. No matter how absurd Bob's phantasy was, the therapist "went him one better." The therapist could climb mightier mountains, swim longer seas, and climb higher trees.

For over a year and a half this type of interchange prevailed until Bob became quite disgusted and said, "You are a bit of a liar, you know. I bet you never did those things. Most of them are impossible anyway. You really lie a lot. Why do you lie so much?" The therapist asked, "What's wrong with lying?" Bob then gave all the reasons for the therapist's lying. "If you really thought you were a big shot, you wouldn't brag so much. You need a psychologist."

The treatment had begun. Bob could start analyzing the therapist's bizarre fantasies (really his own) and attempt to understand their roots. (Strean, 1961, pp. 76–77.)

The personal characteristics which separate orthodox from unorthodox therapists are difficult to specify. One characteristic might be the unorthodox therapist's empathy with the delinquent's battle against social norms. "The psychic situation of the individual is so menaced nowadays by advertisement, propaganda and other more or less well meant advice and suggestions that for once in his life the patient might be offered a relationship that does not repeat the nauseating 'you should,' 'you must' and similar confessions of impotence. Against the onslaught from outside no less than against its repercussions in the psyche of the individual the doctor sees himself obliged to play the role of counsel for the defense" (Jung, 1958, p. 60). Empathy however does not stop at the armchair. Elsewhere, Jung (1953, p. 71) has commented:

The man who would learn the human mind will gain almost nothing from experimental psychology [confined to laboratory measurement]. Far better for him to put away his academic gown, to say good-bye to the study, and to wander with human heart through the world. There, in the horrors of the prison, the asylum, and the hospital, in the drinking-shops, brothels, and gambling halls, in the salons of the elegant, in the exchanges, socialist meetings, churches, religious revivals, and sectarian ecstasies, through love and hate, through the experience of passion in every form in his own body, he would reap a richer store of knowledge than text-books a foot thick could give him. Then would he know how to doctor the sick with real knowledge of the human soul.[10]

A similar willingness to appreciate the life experiences of patients could be found in August Aichhorn—perhaps the most famous of all the therapists who have worked with delinquents—who was, by the way, a mathematician by early training. Kurt Eissler (1956, p. 13) has commented about Aichhorn:

To those who had the privilege of working with him, the most fascinating experience remains the personality of Aichhorn himself. To him work and play coincide. Despite his dedi-

_____

[10] Jung does not object to experimental psychology *per se*, but to limiting experimentation to data obtainable only through instrumentation. "We can see colours but not wave-lengths. This well-known fact must nowhere be more seriously held in view than in psychology. The operation of the personal equation has already begun in the act of observation. One sees what one can best see from oneself. Thus, first and foremost, one sees the mote in one's brother's eye. No doubt the mote is there, but the beam sits in one's own—and may somewhat hinder the act of seeing. I misdoubt the principle of 'pure observation' in so-called objective psychology, unless one confines oneself to the eyepieces of the chronoscope, or to the ergograph and such 'psychological' apparatus. With such methods one also insures oneself against too great a yield of experimental psychological facts." *Psychological Reflections: An Anthology from the Writings of Carl G. Jung*, ed. J. Jacobi (New York: Pantheon, 1953; paperback, Harper Torchbook, 1961, p. 163).

cation to the treatment of delinquents he has never lost his capacity to enjoy the adventure of crime nor his understanding of how sweet to the criminal is the violating of a rule to which the community bows. His faculty for enjoyment is unlimited. A therapeutic success, a well-written mystery story, a ride in a car, a game of cards—for him everything can be an enticing adventure. Thus he is truly young, but spared the hardship of youth, and truly happy because oblivious of his own genius.

With empathy there is often the quality of kindness, a kindness which is symbolic of generosity and strength rather than placation and weakness. It is, if you will permit, a "strategic kindness." Consider, for example, Aichhorn's objective in his Institute for Delinquents at Holla-brunn:

From the very beginning we felt intuitively that above all we must see that the boys and girls from fourteen to eighteen had a good time. We did not treat them as dissocial or criminal individuals from whom society needed protection; they were human beings who had found life too hard, whose antagonism to society was justified, and for whom an environment must be created in which they could feel comfortable. With this attitude as an impetus, the work carried itself along. The faces of the children and the personnel reflected happiness. I can still remember the tension with which we awaited the first admission and how delighted he was when we threw ourselves into the task of winning him over. Later, we modified our treatment in many ways, but I can assure you that even our first exaggerated efforts did no harm. That first boy is well adjusted and has been successfully earning his living for years.

Without really knowing what we were doing we worked out what might be called a practical psychology of reconciliation, which can be used to advantage with most of the children in training institutions at the present time. It is of interest that the same types of delinquency which stirred us to friendliness and kindness provoke the personnel in the older type of institution to an attitude of stern moralism and revenge. I have never felt the need of changing my attitude in this respect but have continued to find it justified. To be sure, there are some delinquents who cannot be influenced by the method outlined above. We shall discuss them later. (Aichhorn, 1935, p. 116.)

How can such kindness be used strategically in the "practical psychology of reconciliation" of which Aichhorn speaks? Aichhorn's description of his treatment of a seventeen-year-old boy who ran away from the institution may provide a partial answer.

At nine o'clock in the evening ten days later, someone knocked on my door. It was the runaway. He was so exhausted physically and under such psychological tension that I felt I could accomplish much more with him than I had planned. I did not reproach him for going away, as he evidently expected. I only looked at him seriously and said, "How long has it been since you had something to eat?" "Yesterday evening." I took him into the dining room of my apartment where my family was at supper and had a place set for him. This boy, who was usually the complete master of a situation, was so upset that he could not eat. Although I was quite aware of this, I said, "Why don't you eat?" "I can't. Couldn't I eat outside?" "Yes, go into the kitchen." His plate was refilled until he was satisfied. When he had finished eating, it was ten o'clock. I went out and said to him, "It's too late for you to go into your group tonight. You can sleep here." A bed was fixed for him in the hall. I patted him on the head and said good-night to him.

The next morning the transference was in effect. He never let himself be led astray after that. He left the institution to become a salesman and for years has had a satisfactory record as a clerk in a business establishment. (Aichhorn, 1935, p. 110.)

Perhaps part of the effectiveness of this kindness is that it is unexpected. The strategy involves the use of surprise as well as consistent interest and enthusiasm.

Ernest Federn (1962, pp. 14–15), in a discussion of the personalities of Paul Federn and August Aichhorn, offers an excellent summary of the unorthodox, therapeutic personality we are attempting to outline here. "In summary, Federn's and Aichhorn's therapeutic personalities may be formulated thus: a combination of strength with kindness, diagnostic skill with therapeutic zeal, scientific objectivity with the gift of empathy. Therapeutic success will always be the greater where one finds these qualities highly developed, because, being opposite poles, they produce the effect of an emotional shock on a patient who comes between them."

For the purpose of statistical analysis, the experimenters in the Streetcorner Research project were placed in the categories of orthodox and unorthodox. The social worker, the social-work student, and the priest were considered orthodox in comparison to the psychologist and the student in education. This judgment was based primarily on the various activities conducted by each experimenter. The orthodox experimenters conducted interviews of a rather standard nature and helped with the driver-trainer program. Activities conducted by the unorthodox experimenters included meeting delinquents on the streetcorner to gain their attendance at the laboratory, card-playing interviews, multiple interviewing, serving free beer at group meetings, and interviewing inside a church.

The unorthodox orientation of the experimenters, which led to the design of the activities cited above, was also apparent in other ways. For example, one of the boys stole a tape recorder from the project. The project had no authority by which it could punish the boy or demand the return of the recorder. Yet something had to be done since this was the first major item stolen from the project. The other boys were eagerly waiting for the results. The psychologist could offer to buy the recorder back, but this would be rewarding the stealing. He could ignore the incident, but this would probably be interpreted by the others as approval of stealing or weakness. Finally, a decision was reached. The psychologist made the general announcement that, "If you need something so badly you have to steal it, we'll help you get it." To prove his point he gave a recorder away to a boy in the project who seemed to enjoy recorders most.

The delinquent ranks were thrown into confusion. Such an action did not fit into their standard view of the world. Mingled with their surprise was the feeling that somehow the boy who had stolen the recorder had been outwitted. He could have had a recorder without the effort and embarrassment of stealing it. The boy who stole the recorder offered to make payments for it, but never completed them before leaving for the service. Much more important, during the group's admiration of the psychologist's maneuver and their surprise, the implicit group norm that nothing should be stolen from the project was reestablished.

When the effectiveness of the orthodox experimenters was compared to the effectiveness of the unorthodox experimenters in the Streetcorner Research project, the unorthodox experimenters were statistically more effective in reducing the number of months of incarceration of the experimental group than the orthodox experimenters. (A discussion of the statistical procedures and results may be found in Appendix C.) It should be remembered that the categories of orthodox and unorthodox are defined here within the context of the Streetcorner Research project. In other contexts, the unorthodox Streetcorner Research experimenter might appear as extremely orthodox; or, conversely, the entire Streetcorner Research project, including the orthodox experimenters, might be considered very unorthodox. The results can only be suggestive of areas for further research.

The importance of the experimenter's personality as a factor in determining the outcome of behavior change techniques based upon changes in the subject's personality cannot be easily dismissed. The characteristics of personality most effective are not yet definitely known. It is likely, however, that in the field of delinquency "all good therapists, whatever their theoretical orientation, have impact rather like the sharp rap of the Zen master" (Levenson, 1961, p. 178).

The psychological laboratory hidden among the green trees on the college campus or the well-appointed study in the quiet suburban home can effectively isolate the psychologist or philosopher from the unkind realities and sufferings of the delinquent world. But once he has seriously entered that world to change it, the many problems which he once viewed at a distance through his television set become his own. The following letter was received from a discouraged mother in Massachusetts:

Could you possibly help me to help my son, before it is too late. It may be already but I must try again or he is lost, since he seems to be incapable of helping himself. In brief, he was a fairly good child until age 15, when he began to be troublesome and since that time until now he has been going from rotten to worse. He is at ———— now for 35 days observation but will be going to court August 24 for sentencing. They say he is not psychotic, but a severe personality problem which they are not equipped to deal with. He will be 20 years old in December and as of now he has ruined any chances of job, friends, even family in this small town of —. So that while I'm hopeful for his release or at least a short sentence I don't know where he can go. He has used up the patience of everyone. Would or could anyone from your group offer any kind of assistance? We asked everyone, lawyers, priest, doctors, they all agree it's a shame. The shame is that I know that underneath the nasty person he has become there was once a good boy for whom I had hopes and I can't reconcile myself to the fact that there is nothing there to save. Perhaps you can do nothing also, but I must try.

If the experimenter answers this letter "yes," he is immediately involved in the life of the family and in questions of research design. If, on the other hand, he chooses to ignore this letter or answer it "No, we cannot at present offer help," he is also involved in that he has decided that his present work is more important than helping this particular boy. Administrative, scientific, and ethical decisions cannot be avoided. This has always been the situation of those who have dealt directly with deviant behavior, but in recent years the psychologist can directly enter the community with the aid of behavioral science and the experimental model. With this experimental model, the experimenter may ask the community members whose behavior is to be changed to help in the design of the behavior-change techniques to be used with them. The following description of the gradual development of an experimental drug treatment may provide an example of a use of the experimental model in the community.

A thirty-three-year-old ex-inmate who had been recently released from prison came to Streetcorner Research asking for help. Tom, also an ex-sailor, had just forged a check and was fearful that he would be returned to prison. His court record indicated that he had spent the last eighteen years of his life in prison on charges of forgery, and that, during these eighteen years, he had never been released from prison more than three weeks before writing an illegal check. With his permission, the experimenter informed the bartender who had received the illegal check that the check would not be honored at the bank and that Streetcorner Research instead would make good the amount of the check. The experimenter then called Tom's employer at a construction company and asked him to deposit fifty dollars each week out of Tom's pay directly in a local bank where a checking account was set up for Tom. This account was a joint account with two names—Tom's actual name and the name that Tom generally used when writing illegal checks. These first steps were considered emergency measures to allow more time for experimentation. Under the pressure of time it was considered easier to make the check-writing behavior legal rather than to change it.

During the next eight weeks Tom wrote forty-three checks, two of which were illegal. These two checks, written to a bartender and gas station attendant one evening while he was drunk, amounted to thirty-five dollars. At the experimenter's suggestion, Tom paid the bartender and gas station attendant the next day in cash and asked them not to press charges as he was going to participate in an experiment to help prevent this from happening again. They agreed to wait for the outcome of the experiment.

It was near this time that the experimenter, interested in learning theory, had read the work of Dent (1955), who used an emetic, apomorphine, in the treatment of alcoholics. Tom, the experimenter, a psychiatrist, and the bartender all met to discuss Dent's work and to design an experiment. It was agreed that syrup of ipecac, a readily available emetic which acts on the vomiting centers of the brain, would be used instead of apomorphine. Tom's agreement with the group was that if he felt like writing a check and was having trouble controlling this behavior, he would call the experimenter and then come to the laboratory to take a moderate dosage of ipecac—just enough to induce a very sick but subvomiting reaction. Unlike many aversion treatments, the object of this procedure would be to negatively condition the *impulse* to write checks rather than negatively condition or punish the check writing behavior itself. (The ineffectiveness of the usual legal corrective procedures may result in part from the fact that punishment follows the legal act. For example, a delinquent's impulse to steal a car is satisfied by stealing a car and although he may be arrested later the impulse to steal has already been positively reinforced by the illegal act. From a learning point of view, the law has probably punished the delinquent's satisfaction from stealing rather than the impulse to steal.)

Tom came to the laboratory to take ipecac five times over a period of eight months. Each time a blank check and a pen was put in front of him while he was in the process of getting sick. These five sessions were admittedly very unpleasant for him, but he chose to go through with them rather than to return to prison. On one occasion the bartender brought Tom to the laboratory. At the time of this writing, nearly three years later, he has not been in further legal difficulty though there have been difficult times when he has written an illegal check and at the last moment torn it up.

The results in this case were possibly the culmination of a number of factors: the joint checking account, the experimental treatment, and the help of interested citizens. This was only the beginning of an experimental program. A much more thorough but still very limited experiment with syrup of ipecac was begun. The next opportunity for an experiment became available when a twenty-three year old college student referred himself to the laboratory for treatment of "homosexual tendencies" because he had heard that the laboratory was interested in developing new behavioral-change techniques. He agreed to participate as an assistant in the designing of an experimental treatment procedure. As an assistant, he was asked to locate every available study he could find on the treatment of homosexuality through the use of conditioning procedures.[11] In addition, he was asked to carry a small, pocket-sized counter with him each day on which he was to record every homosexual and heterosexual impulse as it occured. Finally, he was asked to keep a daily log of sexual activity, fantasies,

11 For example, see Rachman (1961), Herzberg (1945), Lavin, Thorpe, Barker, Blakemore, and Conway (1961), Eysenck (1960), Blakemore, Thorpe, Conway, and Lavin (1963).

and observations. This recording of sexual impulses and activity was done for a period of thirteen months to establish a clear, statistical base-line before the experimental treatment with syrup of ipecac was begun.

The experimental treatment lasted over a period of fourteen weeks and consisted of taking ipecac three times when homosexual impulses were particularly frequent and likely to lead to homosexual behavior, according to his own prediction. On the first two occasions, the ipecac was given in a psychiatrist's office at levels high enough to induce vomiting and the third time he took the ipecac at a subvomiting dosage while in a "gay" bar. For the past year and a half, he has continued to keep a record of sexual impulses and activity which have showed a marked, statistically significant change. He is now married and in his own words, "very content." Not all his homosexual impulses have been eliminated, nor does he want them to be. He does not consider them a problem, but rather, "nostalgic reminders of the past." Although the monthly average of homosexual impulses is continually decreasing, there is no guarantee of success, but it is always possible in case of relapse to repeat the experimental treatment.

Out of successes, partial successes, or even failures, a behavioral technology is gradually developed through the use of scientific methods with the help of those individuals in the community who are interested in the modification of behavior. Many of these people participate as subjects or research assistants, and their daily-life activities produce much of the research data.

It is clear that the movement of experimental methods beyond the confines of the laboratory into the daily-life situations of people will necessitate a clarification of the methods and ethics of experimentation as well as more precise methods of measuring behavior in natural settings. A recent advance in the measurement of behavior in natural settings is the design of a small, portable transmitter called a "Behavior Transmitter-Reinforcer" (BT-R)[12]. The BT-R weighs approximately twenty ounces and is small enough to be easily worn (approximately $7'' \times 4'' \times 2''$). It has a transmitting range of about one-quarter of a mile under adverse city conditions. The BT-R may be integrated with repeater stations and a recording graph at the base station so that there may be an immediate and accurate recording of behavioral events as they occur in the bearer's environment. Thus, a cumulative record of relevant behaviors of a group or person may be obtained over a long period of time. Because the BT-R is also a receiving unit, the person or group may receive signals from the base station, making possible a behavioral feedback system that may have considerable therapeutic potential. Recently, a BT-R unit has been modified and integrated into a series of repeater stations in such a manner that a continuous recording of the wearer's geographical location may be obtained. This is the prototype of an electronic parole and therapy system (Schwitzgebel, Schwitzgebel, Pahnke, and Hurd, 1964).

At the beginning of this section, it was indicated that the psychologist could now in recent years enter the community with the aid of behavioral science and the concept of experimentation. The techniques of behavior change, which then evolve from the use of experimentation in the daily lives of individuals, are the result of the experimenter and these individuals working together. The person whose behavior is to be changed is an expert on his own behavior. He can provide information which is not available in any other way. The mutuality of working together, the honesty required in a collaborative scientific endeavor, and the enthusiasm and optimism inherent in the search for significant

[12] The development of the BT-R is under the direction of the Science Committee on Psychological Experimentation (SCOPE), in Cambridge, Massachusetts.

new knowledge has characterized much of the feeling tone of the Streetcorner Research project. After several years, some guiding principles are beginning to take shape such as the use of a role relation with delinquents which allows them to feel important and the involvement of the delinquent and nondelinquent in tasks which are mutually important to both. A summary of these principles, which may be of some use in designing new programs in other communities, may be found in the conclusion to follow.

The application of the experimental method to the problem of delinquent behavior points the way to the application of this same method to the solution of other human problems as well. This immediately raises the issue of the goals toward which we attempt to change human behavior. Behavioral technology cannot answer that question because the answer lies in the realm of ethics and philosophy from which the scientific method itself is derived.

The great heresy of our age is not the acceptance of scientific knowledge and its fruits, but the assumption that the scientist, *qua* scientist, can help us to choose the good and eschew the evil, that the maker of our machines can be the keeper of our conscience. To avoid this heresy we need to take another look at science and scientists and particularly at our own attitude toward them.

And this is the vital error which we shall find: We, the human race, especially that part of it living in the Western world, have devoted almost all our capacity for scientific thought to the making of machines and to the wresting from nature of the power to put them to work. We have neglected to use our scientific imagination to a comparable degree for studying the minds of those who will decide what the machines will do. We have neglected to use science to solve the problems of environment, of living space, of nervous equanimity, which must be solved if these minds are to be sane enough to use machines sanely. How can we now escape from this one-sided use of our scientific genius? Not certainly by any scientific moratorium, by refusing to learn more lest someone use knowledge for evil ends; but by redressing the balance between our knowledge of machines and our knowledge of human nature. (Langdon-Davies, 1961, p. 22.)

In sum, we need to provide the directions in which science is to grow.

The solution of behavior problems such as delinquency therefore should not be viewed exclusively as a behavioral science endeavor, though such a view is most certainly needed, but also as a task belonging to the arts and philosophy as well. We are still only slowly recovering from the divorce in intellectual history in the 1920's of literature and science. As Hermann Hesse observes in his Nobel Prize novel, *Magister Ludi* (1949), the arts and the sciences are not only opposites but also poles of a single unit. One of Hesse's characters, the Music Master, makes a comment very appropriate to the technical complexities, personal characteristics, and philosophical risk still required in this early stage of experimental-therapeutic crime reduction: "One thing is certain: the game is not without its dangers. And for this very reason we love it, for we send only the weaker ones upon safe paths" (p. 75).

A vision of the future must lie before those who would seek to transform the delinquent into a nobler part of humanity. With the aid of science and philosophy, the future shape of humanity is a goal toward which we strive and whose image and laws are not yet clear. There is still the possibility for a kindly future in which people of violence and cruelty may seem as outmoded as the witches of a previous age. We, therefore, look forward to the time when men shall not only do good, but shall do good measurably well.

Out of the successes and failures of the Streetcorner Research project several guiding principles are beginning to emerge in the therapeutic reduction of adolescent crime. Some of these principles are already well-known and widely used, others are not. The application of only one or two of them alone may not be effective. The greatest effectiveness will probably come from a combination of several of them into a complete system. The following principles are only tentative. They are briefly presented here to encourage further experimentation.

1) To gain cooperation, the delinquent should be explicitly and honestly told about the program and situation in which he is to be involved. Direct and kindly honesty will probably surprise and please him even though he may not be willing to believe completely what is said. The general atmosphere should be one which encourages curiosity, exploration, and the asking of questions. This openness and honesty should set the tone for other activities.

2) There should be a positive relation between the delinquent and the nondelinquent working with him. This relation should include appreciation of the delinquent as a person as well as respect for what he is attempting to accomplish through his inadequate, delinquent behavior.

This means that certain people will probably work better with delinquents than others. The specific characteristics which are most useful are not yet clear. However, some clues may be found in Ernest Federn's (1962) description of the therapeutic personality, based upon the personalities of Paul Federn and August Aichhorn, as "a combination of strength with kindness, diagnostic skill with therapeutic zeal, scientific objectivity with the gift of empathy." A successful delinquency program probably cannot be achieved without a consideration of the personalities involved.

3) The formal role relation between the delinquent and the nondelinquent should be socially acceptable to both. Ideally, the delinquent should be placed in a role which gives him prestige both from his own viewpoint and the viewpoint of the community. Some of these roles might be team member, experimental-research subject, apprentice, office assistant, and so forth. These roles permit the boy to learn about other styles of life without the embarrassment which is attached to the role of patient or parolees.

4) The delinquent and the nondelinquent should be involved in a mutually important task which is not exclusively the elimination of the delinquent's illegal behavior. This task may be winning a baseball game, building a sports car, collecting psychological data, or some other project which actively involves both participants. "Getting the job done" must be important to both participants.

Under these conditions, the delinquent and the nondelinquent will continue to work together even when the personal relation between them is not ideal. The delinquent will continue to cooperate, for example, even though he is angry with the coach, if both he and the coach are eager to win a game. Also, the coach is more likely to be considerate of the delinquent if he is a valuable player. This is very much different from programs which are designed primarily "for the good of the delinquent," such as craft programs in which it is not personally important to the leader whether the delinquent completes his task or not.

5) The role relation should include time for the delinquent and the nondelinquent to talk together and share important feelings. The amount of time spent talking to-

gether, what is said, and how the personal relation is developed may be designed according to what the leader believes is most beneficial in reducing the delinquent behavior. Under these conditions, therapy, work, and play are not necessarily separate activities. Their combination may prove very effective.

6) The nondelinquent should be somewhat older, perhaps, but not considerably older than the delinquent. He should also be employed in some trade or profession which is a feasible occupation for the delinquent to enter. In this way, the nondelinquent serves as a role model which the delinquent may imitate while learning for himself new patterns of behavior.

7) Finally, a delinquency program should be conducted enthusiastically and with constant evaluation as to its effectiveness in reaching specific, well-defined goals.

There are probably many perspectives from which delinquency prevention projects may effectively operate. The Streetcorner Research project represents one of these perspectives. The critically important factor, however, in developing increasingly effective programs in the future is the application of scientific principles. This will require setting up clear, measurable objectives, explicitly defining the procedures, and then carefully evaluating the results. Under these conditions, and the consequent social safeguards, a wide range of new, creative behavioral techniques may be safely applied to the problems of delinquency. There is still good reason for optimism.

Appendices

APPENDIX A. RESULTS OF STREETCORNER RESEARCH PROJECT IN CAMBRIDGE

Criteria	Subjects									
	Art	Bill	Chuck	Dave	Ed	Frank	George	Hugh	Ike	
Age at time of employment by project	16	16	18	21	15	19	17	15	20	1
Years of school completed	10	10	8	10	10	10	9	8	10	1
Barred from community services	no	yes	yes	yes	no	yes	no	yes	no	n
Attitude toward treatment[a]	R	R	R	H	R	R	R	CT	H	D
Attendance at laboratory[b]	D	D	D	D	D	D	D	D	D	V
Before association with the laboratory:										
Months of full-time work	0	1	0	36	2	0	0	0	0	
Gang membership	yes	yes	yes	no	yes	yes	yes	yes	yes	ye
Number of arrests	4	14	9	7	16	12	10	20	9	
Number of court appearances	4	6	5	1	4	4	5	6	4	
Months sentenced (cumulative)	30	38	54	6	30	24	30	48	25	
Months in reform school	15	12	10	0	12	3	22	14	12	
Months in adult prison	0	0	0	6	0	8	0	0	0	
After association with the laboratory:										
Months of full-time work[c]	25	7	13	14	$20\frac{1}{2}$	13	24	0	4	3
Gang membership	no	no	yes	no	no	no	no	no	no	n
Number of arrests[d]	2	4	6	2	1	1	2	13	6	-
Number of court appearances[d]	2	4	1	2	—	1	1	5	4	-
Months sentenced (cumulative)[d]	12	42	—	18	—	6	6	30	12	-
Months in reform school[d]	—	—	—	—	—	—	—	—	—	-
Months in adult prison[d]	—	12	—	8	—	—	—	15	12	-

[a] R (active refusal); H (expressed hostility); DT (desired treatment); CT (cooperated treatment).
[b] D (daily); W (weekly); L (less than weekly).

		Subjects																	
	Len	Mike	Neal	Otto	Pete	Quent	Ralph	Sam	Ted	Vic	Walt	Andy	Ben	Chet	Dan	Eric	Glenn	Harry	John
6	18	20	18	16	20	18	19	19	20	16	16	17	17	20	19	18	21	20	16
0	10	10	11	8	10	10	12	10	12	12	12	10	9	12	8	12	10	8	10
o	yes	no	no	no	no	no	no	yes	no	no	no	no	no	no	yes	no	no	no	yes
I	R	H	H	R	DT	H	H	R	H	H	H	H	H	CT	R	R	R	R	CT
)	W	L	W	D	W	W	D	L	L	L	D	L	L	L	W	L	D	D	D
3	6	12	0	0	17	3	0	6	0	0	3	0	0	12	0	8	0	3	0
s	yes	yes	no	yes	no	no	yes	no	no	yes	yes	yes	yes	yes	no	no	yes	yes	yes
6	5	5	0	5	3	3	1	5	0	2	5	0	1	0	18	0	1	3	4
3	3	2	0	4	2	2	1	2	0	1	2	0	1	0	5	0	1	1	2
2	12	6	0	44	22	12	6	12	0	6	9	0	4	0	24	0	6	6	12
6	0	0	0	36	18	0	0	0	0	0	6	0	0	0	12	0	0	19	8
0	6	0	0	0	1	6	0	9	0	0	0	0	0	0	6	0	0	47	0
9	31	30	15	12	34	14	21	31	25	16	16	36	32	28	7	23	47	22	17
o	no	no	no	no	no	no	no	no	no	no	yes	yes	no	no	no	no	no	yes	no
1	—	1	2	1	2	—	—	1	—	—	—	—	—	—	3	—	—	1	1
-	—	1	—	1	2	—	—	1	—	1	—	—	—	—	3	—	—	1	—
-	—	—	—	12	12	—	—	6	—	—	—	—	—	—	18	—	—	24	—
-	—	—	—	—	—	—	—	—	—	—	—	—	—	—	—	—	—	—	—
-	—	—	—	—	2	—	—	—	—	—	—	—	—	—	8	—	—	12	—

This information is correct insofar as were able to determine.
The dash indicates no arrests, court appearances, months sentenced or served, according to available information.

Subject[a]	Age at first offense	Nation-ality	Type of offense	City of residence	Months in reform school[b]	Months in prison[b]	No. of arrests[c]	Months in reform school[c]	Mont[hs] in pris[on]
Art	12.0	Irish	P & P[d]	Cambridge	15	0	2	—e	—
Control	11.6	Irish	P & P	Cambridge	17	0	2	—	—
Bill	12.5	English	P & P	Cambridge	12	0	4	—	12
Control	12.3	English	P & P	Cambridge	16	0	2	—	3
Chuck	14.8	Italian	P & P	Cambridge	10	0	6	—	—
Control	14.6	Italian	P & P	Cambridge	8	0	4	—	—
Dave	15.1	English	Property	Cambridge	0	6	2	—	8
Control	15.5	English	Property	Cambridge	10	0	—	—	—
Ed	13.0	English	P & P	Cambridge	12	0	1	—	—
Control	13.3	English	P & P	Cambridge	15	0	—	—	—
Frank	14.2	Italian	P & P	Cambridge	3	8	1	—	—
Control	14.3	Italian	P & P	Cambridge	13	0	7	—	11
George	15.2	Irish	P & P	Cambridge	22	0	2	—	—
Control	14.9	Irish	Person	Cambridge	18	0	21	—	19
Hugh	10.1	Unknown	P & P	Cambridge	14	0	13	—	15
Control	10.8	Irish	P & P	Cambridge	6	7	11	—	18
Ike	14.11	English	Person	Cambridge	12	0	6	—	12
Control	14.8	English	Property	Boston	8	0	2	—	12
Joe	13.8	Italian	Property	Cambridge	6	0	—	—	—
Control	13.11	Italian	Property	Cambridge	6	0	4	—	—
Karl	14.8	Unknown	Property	Cambridge	6	0	1	—	—
Control	14.9	Italian	Property	Boston	6	0	1	—	—
Len	15.1	English	P & P	Cambridge	0	6	—	—	—
Control	15.3	English	P & P	Cambridge	0	10	5	—	—
Otto	14.0	Irish	P & P	Cambridge	36	0	1	—	—
Control	13.7	Irish	P & P	Cambridge	25	0	4	—	18
Pete	8.9	English	P & P	Cambridge	18	1	2	—	2
Control	8.10	Italian	P & P	Cambridge	21	0	2	—	—
Quent	13.0	English	Property	Cambridge	0	6	—	—	—
Control	13.2	English	Property	Cambridge	0	8	6	—	—
Sam	15.2	Italian	P & P	Cambridge	0	9	1	—	—
Control	15.8	Unknown	P & P	Cambridge	8	3	4	—	13
Walt	13.3	Irish	Property	Cambridge	6	0	—	—	—
Control	13.6	Irish	Property	Boston	6	0	3	—	—
Dan	14.8	Irish	P & P	Cambridge	12	6	3	—	8
Control	15.0	English	P & P	Cambridge	10	6	—	—	—
Henry	15.1	English	P & P	Boston	19	47	1	—	1
Control	15.0	English	P & P	Boston	7	60	10	—	24
John	14.3	Irish	Property	Somerville	8	0	1	—	—
Control	14.1	Irish	P & P	Somerville	0	12	5	—	19

a Only the 20 boys who served time in reform school or prison are matched.
b Before February 15, 1959.
c After February 15, 1959, through February 15, 1962.
d P & P stands for person and property.
e The dash indicates no arrests or months served according to available information.

A. *Structure of experimental and control groups.* The experimental group consisted of thirty white males from the Cambridge-Boston area employed by Streetcorner Research for six months or longer. Of these thirty boys, twenty-five were known to the court and twenty had spent six months or more in a correctional institution. The twenty boys who had been incarcerated presented the following mean characteristics: age 17.8 at the time of their employment by the project; 9.6 years of school completed; 3.9 months of full-time work; 8.2 arrests; 3.4 court appearances; 10.6 months in reform school; 4.5 months in adult prison.

Thirteen of the twenty boys who had been incarcerated were estimated to have come from a lower-lower socioeconomic background, one from a lower-middle socioeconomic background, and two from an upper middle socioeconomic background. Six were of Irish parentage, four Italian, eight English, and two undetermined by this study. Eleven stated their religious preference as Catholic, five as Protestant, and four no preference. Fifteen were gang members, nine had been barred from community services such as settlement houses, and eleven had histories of active refusal to participate in treatment programs. A detailed description of each subject may be found in Appendix A.

A control group was formed by matching each member of the experimental group with a male offender chosen from the records of the Department of Probation and Parole and the Youth Service Board, Commonwealth of Massachusetts. Data from these sources was supplemented by data from the Cambridge Crime Prevention Bureau, the Boston Crime Prevention Bureau, and the Cambridge Neighborhood House. The pairs were matched as nearly as possible on age of first offense, nationality, type of offense (person and/or property), city of residence, and time spent in reform school and prison prior to February 1959.

The mean age of first offense for the experimental group was 13.6 years, for the control group 13.7. The mean number of months incarcerated before February 15, 1959, for the experimental group was 15.0, for the control group 15.3. Specific pairings on these variables may be found in Appendix B.

The pairs were not matched according to the amount of school completed, socioeconomic class, refusal to participate in treatment, or whether they had been barred from community services. Since 65 percent of the experimental group were estimated to have come from lower-lower socioeconomic backgrounds, 55 percent had histories of refusal to participate in treatment, and 45 percent had been barred from community services, it can be expected that the population from which the experimental group was drawn may be somewhat more resistant to improvement than the control group population. Thus, these specifically unmatched characteristics are expected to weigh the data against significant experimental results.

B. *Comparison of experimental and control groups on rates of crime.* The following null hypothesis was tested: The amount of crime committed by the experimental group does not show a significant decrease as measured by various indices when compared to a matched-pair control group on these same indices *before* (T-1) and *after* (T-2) employment of the experimental group by the Streetcorner Research project. The indices used to measure the amount of crime committed by the experimental and the control groups are 1) number of accumulated arrests, 2) number of incarcerations (recidivism rate), and 3) number of accumulated months of incarceration.

The mean number of arrests for the experimental group three years after their employment was 2.4; the mean number of arrests for the control group over an equivalent period of time was 4.7. The Wilcoxon matched-pairs signed-ranks test (Siegel, 1956) was used to test the null hypothesis which was subsequently rejected ($\propto < .025$; $T = 33.0$).

During the three-year follow-up period, seven (or 35 percent) of the experimental group were incarcerated. During the same period, nine (or 45 percent) of the control group were incarcerated. This difference did not reach the $\alpha = .05$ level of significance ($\chi^2 = 20.86$). Therefore, using the number of persons incarcerated as an index, the null hypothesis was accepted.

One of the most important indices of crime for the project was the number of months of incarceration accumulated by the experimental and control groups. The mean number of months of incarceration of the experimental group three years after employment was 3.5. The mean number of months of incarceration of the control group over the same period of time was 6.9. The following table shows the months of incarceration for both groups. The assumption of equality of population variances was tested and the data were found to be insufficient to warrant rejection of the null hypothesis ($t = .02$, $\alpha < .10$).

Pair-group	Experimental Subject	Control Subject
1	0	0
2	12	3
3	0	0
4	8	0
5	0	0
6	0	11
7	0	19
8	15	18
9	12	12
10	0	0
11	0	0
12	0	0
13	0	18
14	2	0
15	0	0
16	0	13
17	0	0
18	8	0
19	12	24
20	0	19

Note: Figures given in this table are based on a follow-up period from February 1959 to February 1962.

With the additional assumption of normal distribution, a t-test was used to determine whether the difference between the two means of the correlated samples was significant. The null hypothesis was rejected ($t = 7.79$, $\propto\ < .05$). Therefore, on this index of months of incarceration, the experimental group showed a significant reduction in the amount of committed crime as compared to the control group. Thus, it may be concluded on the basis of two of the three indices that the experimental group gives evidence of a significant reduction in the amount of known crime in comparison to the control group.

The failure of the experimental group, however, to show a significant reduction in the number of subjects returned to prison, while showing a significant reduction in the number of arrests and months of incarceration for these same subjects, raises several interesting questions. One of these questions is the validity of the data. We would expect three indices sampling the same supposed crime rate of the groups to agree. They do, in fact, agree to the extent that all show a tendency in the same direction, but the decrease in the number of experimental subjects returned to prison does not reach significance at the .05 level. Perhaps this is, in part, a result of the fact that the return rate to prison is a less sensitive measure than the measures of the number of arrests or the number of months incarcerated.

A closer examination of the data indicates that two additional types of biases tend to weight the data against experimental findings. These might be called the "biases of friendship" and the "biases of information." The bias of friendship may enter the data when a project grows naturally within the community as did the Streetcorner Research project, rather than being designed initially with consideration for measurement problems. Ideally, at the beginning of the project twenty matched pairs of boys, randomly selected and meeting the criteria, should have been designated and then one boy from each pair randomly assigned to the experimental group or control group. Instead, the control group was selected after the formation of the experimental group. As the experimental group developed, subjects told their friends about the project and some of these friends were later selected as subjects. Consequently, the experimental group probably contains more natural friendships than an experimental group to which subjects would be randomly assigned.

At least one bias caused by these friendships in the experimental group may be reflected in the follow-up data. Friends tend to commit crimes together, and thus arrests and incarcerations for a particular crime are likely to affect a larger percentage of the experimental group than the control group. For example, subjects Pete and Dan and a third friend were involved in the theft of a cab. This one act contributed two arrests and two incarcerations to the experimental group. Another example was the arrest of subjects Hugh and Ike for drunkenness while they were out together one night. It might be argued on the other hand that when one friend no longer engages in crime it will keep the other out of trouble, but evidence for this is slight. More often it appears from our experience that the friendship breaks up.

Another factor which may weight the data against experimental findings is the "bias of information." In this study, this bias is a result of maintaining contact with the experimental subjects (either directly or through their friends and relatives) while there was no such contact with the controls. Therefore, the follow-up study of the experimental group includes arrests and incarcerations which do not appear on official records whereas the arrests and incarcerations of the control group are only those appearing on official records. This is of considerable importance as many of the experimental group, and possibly many of the control group, were out of the state for varying periods of time. The inadequacy of official recording, particularly between states, is well-known. Note, for example, the "absurdity" that Virginia reports having only a 13.7 percent recidivism rate while West Virginia reports 51.1 percent and California reports 75 percent (Bennett, 1954, p. 10). At least eight arrests and two out-of-state incarcerations of the experimental group did not appear on Massachusetts records. Thus, the recidivism rate of the experimental group based only on state records of incarceration would have been 25 percent rather than the "known" 35 percent. This "bias of information" might also be called the "bias of ignorance" to the extent that it operates to minimize the crime rate of the control group.

These biases raise the whole issue of the relation of recorded and known crime to the amount of crime actually committed. With little doubt, the experimental group committed many more crimes than are shown on official records or personally reported. This same condition probably holds true for the control group. V. W. Peterson, Operating Director of the Chicago Crime Commission, notes that over a six-month period in 1948 in Chicago only 137 out of 1576 shoplifting cases were reported to the police (Taft, 1956, p. 63). In a counseling project with delinquency-prone boys in the Cambridge-Somerville, Massachusetts area, there were only 27 court complaints (6 percent) on 4400 minor offenses and 68 complaints (11 percent) on 616 serious felony offenses (Murphy, Shirley and Witner, 1946). See Cressey (1957) and Schwartz (1946) for a further discussion of this problem.

C. Comparison of the experimental group to a general rate of delinquency. Early in the formulation of these findings, it was decided to compare the known crime rate of the experimental group *before* and *after* their employment by the project in order to determine whether there was a significant change. However, it soon became apparent that a significant change in the experimental group was meaningful only if it was compared to the change which could be expected to occur without intervention. For example, if the rate of incarceration of the experimental group was reduced by 50 percent, would this be significant if a 30 percent reduction was generally expected? The writer thus set out to determine the *expected* recidivism rate of the experimental group if there had been no intervention. This rate would then be used as a base for determining significant change.

The establishment of an expected recidivism rate for this particular group, based on observations of similar groups in society, turned out to be an almost impossible task. Nevertheless, when people are told that the recidivism rate of the experimental group is 35 percent, there is an inevitable evaluation of results which ranges from "good," or "fair," to "poor." Any one of these evaluations suggests an implicit standard of expected recidivism. The problems involved in establishing recidivism rates and the range of recorded recidivism in Massachusetts may be of some interest.

One of the most frequently cited studies of recidivism in Massachusetts is a study done by the Division of Legal Medicine, Massachusetts Department of Mental Health, which found that 67 percent of 546 men given parole in 1952 were either parole violators, convicted of new crime while on parole, or convicted of new crime within a five-year period following release from prison (Shapiro, Cohen and Bugden, 1959). The recidivism rate for adult, male felony offenders over a five-year period generally ranges from 50 to 70 percent in most states with a nation-wide average of 66.6 percent (Mattick, 1960, p. 54). Eleanor and Sheldon Glueck (1949, p. 17) report a 60.5 recidivism rate for the Massachusetts Reformatory for a five-year period, while Sutherland and Cressey (1960, p. 591) note that about 72 percent of the offenders admitted to the prison reformatories of Massachusetts in 1957 had been previously incarcerated. Related findings can be found in Bennett (1954), Vold (1954), State of New York (1949), Zuckerman, Barron, and Whittier (1953), and the United States Department of Justice (1960).

In a control of 18 boys for the Cambridge-Somerville project in Massachusetts, 33 percent of those boys who went to reform school were later sentenced to prison (McCord, McCord and Zola, 1959). Arbuckle and Litwack (1960) studied the recidivism of a group of 100 boys randomly selected from the population of the Lyman School for Boys in Westboro, Massachusetts (an "open" institution without walls or fences). At the end of a 17-month waiting period, 35 percent had been returned to a training school. The Gluecks (1940, pp. 1, 35, 86–88) reported that 73.1 percent of 67 boys from the Boston area who had been incarcerated were again imprisoned within a five-year follow-up period between the years of 1917 and 1922. Recidivism rates for juvenile parolees throughout the country generally range from 43 to 73 percent (Arbuckle and Litwack, 1960, p. 45).

It should be clear that no one study cited here has defined a group specifically enough to establish an expected recidivism rate for our experimental group. No single study considers the many possible critical variables as age, years during which the study was conducted, geographical location, time incarcerated, type of offense, ethnic background, socioeconomic class, and so forth. Only inferences from a comparison of these studies can suggest a range of expected recidivism for the experimental group.

The lowest recidivism rate for juvenile offenders in Massachusetts was 33 percent (McCord, McCord and Zola, 1959), but this group was much younger than the experimental group and had much less extended and severe records. These same differences hold for the Arbuckle and Litwack group (1960) which showed a 35 percent recidivism rate for boys attending an "open" institution. None of the experimental group attended an open institution and at least 40 percent of the experimental group served adult time.

The juvenile group most characteristic of the experimental group is that of the Gluecks (1940, p. 19), which had a recidivism rate of 73.1 percent. But this rate is too high to be an expected rate for the experimental group because the mean age of the group studied by the Gluecks was younger than the experimental group despite the fact that they served an approximately equal amount of time in correctional institutions. Holding the length of incarceration constant, the study by Arbuckle and Litwack (1960) suggests that the older the boy is at the time of parole (up through the age of seventeen), the more likely he is to succeed. Also, the Gluecks studied a group of boys who appeared in court between the years of 1917 and 1922. The effect of this considerable time difference between the Gluecks' study and current studies is difficult to estimate.

Recidivism rates for adult offenders in Massachusetts range from 60.5 percent (Glueck and Glueck, 1949) to approximately 72 percent (Sutherland and Cressey, 1960). Although the mean age of the offenders in these studies is considerably older than the mean age of the adult offenders in the experimental group, we cannot automatically conclude that the recidivism for older adult offenders should be higher than the rate for younger adult offenders. Rather, though the evidence is conflicting, there is some indication that recidivism declines with increasing age (Sellin, 1958; Rumney and Murphy, 1952, pp. 164, 167–168).

Finally, we should note that the recidivism rates of most of the above studies are derived from five-year follow-up periods or longer. The follow-up study of the experimental group is for a three-year period. The distribution of recidivism is disproportional over time. There is a tendency for recidivism to occur, predominantly during the first two years of parole with only slight to moderate increases in the total percentage during the next three years (United States Department of Justice, 1960, p. 39).

Some of the difficulties in establishing an expected recidivism rate for the experimental group from studies in the literature should be clear. One may say, however, that the expected recidivism rate for the experimental group over a five-year period lies somewhere between 33 percent (lowest cited rate for juveniles in Massachusetts) to 72 percent (highest cited rate for adults in Massachusetts). The recidivism rates for groups most nearly corresponding to the experimental group (ignoring the 73.1 percent found by the Gluecks in 1922 because of the time factor) lie in the upper part of the range between 50 and 65 percent. Allowing for a generous 10 percent increase in recidivism for the experimental group during the final two years of the five-year period, the current range of expected recidivism would be 40 to 55 percent. The recidivism of the matched-pari control group was 45 percent and therefore clearly within this range. As discussed in a previous section, however, this rate is probably somewhat low because neither the control group nor the groups cited in the literature were explicitly composed of a majority of subjects who came from a lower-lower socioeconomic background and had actively refused treatment. A closer specification of the expected recidivism rate of the experimental group from the above-cited data would be quite speculative.

D. Results produced by orthodox and unorthodox orientations and various experimental procedures. For the purpose of this investigation, the experimenters were placed in the categories of "orthodox" and "unorthodox," and the experimental procedures were divided into the three categories of "interview," "activity," and "interview and activity." The rating of experimenters as orthodox or unorthodox was based on the observation that the unorthodox experimenters displayed behaviors which were less in keeping with social norms than the orthodox experimenters, and that these behaviors were widely enough distributed through all of the experimenter's work that they suggested a personal orientation of the experimenter. The other experimenters were skillful within their own modes of operation but, in comparison, could be seen as orthodox. Clearly, such a rating of experimenters applies only within the project since the entire project itself could be considered unorthodox from the general viewpoint of the community.

The division of experimental procedures into "interviewing," "activities," and "interviewing and activities" was done on the following basis. "Interviewing" consisted of individual interviews, multiple interviewing, and group discussions led by an experimenter. "Activities" consisted of driver training and building electronic equipment. The category of "interviewing and activities" consisted of a combination of interviewing and activities as described previously, such as card-playing interviews. The subjects were not assigned to procedures or experimenters according to any explicit plan, and there is no evidence that their assignment was not at least as random as the assignment of cases in usual clinical practice.

To help determine the influence of the various procedures and experimenters and their interaction effects on the experimental group, a two-way analysis of variance was used. The entries in the cells of the following table consist of the difference in months of incarceration for each subject before and after employment by the project. For example, Quent, interviewed by an experimenter, spent six months *less* in prison after seeing the experimenter than before and is therefore entered as −6 in cell 11. The time between the first incarceration of the subjects and their employment by the project (T-1) is presumed to be roughly equal to the three-year follow-up period after their employment (T-2). The mean difference between the mean age of first offense of the subjects and the mean age of their employment by the project is 3.7 years, eliminating one case, Peter, whose difference between age of first offense and age of employment was 11.4. Since age of first offense is based upon the age of the first recorded arrest available and since most youths are not incarcerated on first offense, we assume that the mean age of first incarceration is at least several months nearer to the mean age of employment than the mean age of first offense.

Orientation	Procedures		
	Interviewing	Activities	Interviewing and Activities
Orthodox	−6	−9	−16
	−10	−6	−6
	+1		−6
	0		
Unorthodox	−15	−6	0
	−11	−8	−10
	−22		+2
			−12
			−36
			−54

The unequal number of observations per cell is handled by converting the observations in each cell to a cell mean according to Walker and Lev (1953, pp. 316, 351, 381–382). The analysis of variance indicates no significant interaction effect between columns and rows, that is, between orientation and procedures. Only the rows reach a significance level below .05.

Source	Estim.	Sum of Sqs.	df	Means Sq.	F	a
Rows	S^2_r	474.4	1	474.4	5.9	<.05
Cols.	S^2_c	184.3	2	92.3	—	—
Int., A.	S^2_{rc}	90.4	2	45.2	—	—
Error	S^2_w	——	14	80.4	—	—

Statistical examination thus suggests that the unorthodox orientation was more effective than the orthodox orientation in reducing the number of months of incarceration of the experimental group. The various procedures did not produce significant differences between themselves either within or across the categories of orthodox and unorthodox orientation.

It should be remembered that each of the experimental procedures is made up of several subprocedures. For example, the procedure categorized as interviewing consists of individual interviewing, multiple interviewing, and group discussions. Because the effectiveness of these individual subprocedures could not be determined from the small number of subjects to which they were applied, it is impossible to know whether they were of equal effectiveness or whether less effective subprocedures cancelled out the effects of more effective ones.

The analysis of variance further suggests that the various experimental procedures taken together were more effective in combination with the experimenters of an unorthodox orientation than in combination with experimenters of an orthodox orientation. There was no significant difference between the individual procedures of interviewing, activities, and interviewing and activities when carried out by orthodox experimenters compared to unorthodox experimenters. It cannot, therefore, be said that either the orthodox or unorthodox experimenters were more effective in using any particular procedure. It can only be suggested that the unorthodox experimenters were generally more effective across various procedures.

Also, it may be noted that the generalizability of the results obtained in this study may be somewhat more restricted than usual. Not only do the usual limitations of population characteristics, geographical location, time, and so forth, apply but also the condition that all procedures were carried out within the experimenter-subject role relation. The extent to which another role relation might have modified the varying effectiveness of orthodox-unorthodox orientations is unknown.

E. Summary. The experimental group showed a significant reduction in the number of arrests ($\alpha < .025$) and in the number of months of incarceration ($\propto < .05$) over a three-year follow-up period in comparison to a matched-pair control group. The less sensitive index of number of persons incarcerated (recidivism) showed a tendency in the same direction but did not reach significance below the .05 level.

The factors of friendships within the experimental group and of more accurate information about experimental subjects' arrests and incarcerations were discussed as biases usually operating against obtaining significant differences in favor of the experimental group. A few problems relative to establishing a general expected base-rate of recidivism for the experimental group were also discussed. The conclusion was reached that a fairly conservative estimate would allow a base-rate of expected recidivism between 40 and 55 percent. The recidivism rate for the control group fell within this range at 45 percent.

A difference in the amount of improvement *within* the experimental group was noted. The significant factor in this improvement appeared to be an orthodox or unorthodox approach of the experimenter regardless of specific procedures he might have used with his subjects. The over-all context of the work remained within the experimenter-subject role relation. What effect, if any, a different role would have on the results of an orthodox or unorthodox personal orientation is open to future investigation.

Bibliography

Bibliography

Aichhorn, A., *Wayward Youth* (New York: Viking, 1935; paperback, Meridian Books, 1957).

Alexander, F., "Unexplored Areas in Psychoanalytic Theory and Treatment," *Behavioral Science* 3:293–316 (1958).

American Medical Association, "Supplementary Report of the Judicial Council of the American Medical Association," *Journal of the American Medical Association* 132:1090 (1946).

Appel, K. E., "Presidential Address: The Challenge of Psychiatry," *American Journal of Psychiatry* 3:1–12 (1954).

Arbuckle, D. S., "Counseling: Philosophy or Science," *Personnel and Guidance Journal* 39:11–14 (1960).

———— and L. Litwack, "A Study of Recidivism among Juvenile Delinquents," *Federal Probation* 24:45–48 (1960).

Atkinson, R. C., G. R. Sommer, and M. B. Sterman, "Decision-Making by Children as a Function of Amount of Reinforcement," *Psychological Reports* 6:299–306 (1960).

Ayllon, T., "Intensive Treatment of Psychotic Behavior by Stimulus Satiation and Food Reinforcement," *Behaviour Research and Therapy* 1:53–61 (1963).

Azrin, N. H., and O. R. Lindsley, "The Reinforcement of Cooperation between Children," *Journal of Abnormal and Social Psychology* 52:100–102 (1956).

Bandura, A., D. Ross, and S. A. Ross, "Transmission of Aggression through Imitation of Aggressive Models," *Journal of Abnormal and Social Psychology* 63:575–582 (1961).

Barker, R. G., and H. F. Wright, *The Midwest and Its Children: The Psychological Ecology of an American Town* (Evanston, Ill.: Row, Peterson, 1954).

Bazelon, D. L., "The Imperative to Punish," Brandeis Lecture, Brandeis University, Waltham, Mass., 1961 (unpublished).

Beecher, H. W., *Experimentation in Man* (Springfield, Ill.: Thomas, 1958).

Bennett, J. V., "Evaluating a Prison," *Annals of the American Academy of Political and Social Science* 293:10–16 (1954).

Betz, B. J., and J. C. Whitehorn, "The Relationship of the Therapist to the Outcome of Therapy in Schizophrenia," *Psychiatric Research Report*, no. 5 (1956).

Blakemore, C. B., J. G. Thorpe, J. C. Barker, C. G. Conway, and N. I. Lavin, "The Application of Faradic Aversion Conditioning in a Case of Transvestism," *Behaviour Research and Therapy* 1:29–34 (1963).

Bromberg, W., "Dynamic Aspects of Psychopathic Personality," *Psychoanalytic Quarterly* 17:58–70 (1948).

Bruner, J. S., *On Knowing: Essays for the Left Hand* (Cambridge, Mass.: Harvard University Press, 1962).

Buber, Martin, *Between Man and Man* (Boston: Beacon Press, 1957).

Chein, J., S. W. Cook, and J. Harding, "The Use of Research in Social Therapy," *Human Relations* 1:497–511 (1948).

Cherry, C., and B. McA. Sayers, "Experiments upon the Total Inhibition of Stammering by External Controls and Some Clinical Results," *Journal of Psychosomatic Research* 49:508–512 (1954).

Cressey, D. R., "The State of Criminal Statistics," *National Probation and Parole Association Journal* 3:230–241 (1957).

De Grazia, S., *Errors of Psychotherapy* (New York: Doubleday, 1952).

Dent, J. Y., *Anxiety and Its Treatment* (London: Skeffington, 1955).

Department of Social Relations, Harvard University, "Code Governing the Use of Students as Subjects in Research," mimeographed (1960).

Devereux, G., and F. H. Hoffman, "Non-recognition of the Patient by the Therapist," *Psychoanalysis and Psychoanalytic Review* 48:41–61 (1961).

Dinoff, M., H. C. Rickhard, H. Saltzberg, and C. H. Sipprelle, "An Experimental Analogue of Three Psychotherapeutic Approaches," *Journal of Clinical Psychology* 16:70–73 (1960).

Doolittle, H., *Tribute to Freud* (New York: Pantheon, 1956).

Eissler, K. R., "Ego-Psychological Implication of the Psychoanalytic Treatment of Delinquents," in *The Psychoanalytic Study of the Child*, vol. V (New York: International Universities Press, 1950).

——— ed., *Searchlights on Delinquency* (New York: International Universities Press, 1956).

Erikson, C., W. Kuethe, and D. Sullivan, "Some Personality Correlates of Learning without Verbal Awareness," *Journal of Personality* 26:216–228 (1958).

Eysenck, H. J., ed., *Behaviour Therapy and the Neuroses* (London: Pergamon Press, 1960).

Federn, E., "The Therapeutic Personality, as Illustrated by Paul Federn and August Aichhorn," *The Psychiatric Quarterly* (published by the New York State Department of Mental Hygiene, Utica, N.Y.), January 1962, pp. 1–15.

Fenichel, O., "Some Remarks on Freud's Place in the History of Science," *The Collected Papers of Otto Fenichel* (New York: Norton, 1954), pp. 362–366.

Fiedler, F. E., "Quantitative Studies on the Role of Therapists' Feelings toward Their Patients," in O. H. Mowrer, ed., *Psychotherapy: Theory and Research* (New York: Ronald Press, 1953), pp. 296–315.

Fine, R., "The Measurement Problem in Psychology," *Psychoanalysis and Psychoanalytic Review* 47:91–105 (1960).

Fowler, W., "Teaching a Two-Year-Old to Read: An Experiment in Early Childhood Learning," *Genetic Psychology Monographs* 66:181–183 (1962).

Frank, J. D., *Persuasion and Healing: A Comparative Study of Psychotherapy* (Baltimore: Johns Hopkins Press, 1961).

Franks, C. M., "Recidivism, Psychopathy, and Personality," *British Journal of Delinquency* 6:192–201 (1956).

Freud, S., *Collected Papers*, ed., E. Jones (New York: Basic Books, 1959).

Friedman, J. H., "Short-term Psychotherapy of 'Phobia of Travel,'" *American Journal of Psychotherapy* 4:259–278 (1950).

Frym, M., "The Treatment of Recidivists," *Journal of Criminal Law, Criminology, and Police Science* 47:1–7 (1956).

Geddes, D. P., ed., *An Analysis of the Kinsey Reports on Sexual Behavior in the Human Male and Female* (New York: Dutton, 1954; paperback, Mentor, 1954).

Glover, E., "Psycho-analysis and Criminology: A Political Survey," *International Journal of Psychoanalysis* 37:311–317 (1956).

Glueck, S., and E. Glueck, *Juvenile Delinquents Grown Up* (New York: Commonwealth Fund, 1940).

—— *After-Conduct of Discharged Offenders* (New York: Oxford University Press, 1949).

Goldsmith, A. O., "Challenges of Delinquency to Casework Treatment," *Social Work*, April 1959, pp. 14–19.

Grandy, J. M., "Preventive Work with Street-Corner Groups: Hyde Park Youth Project, Chicago," in *Annals of the American Academy of Political and Social Science* 322:107–116 (1959).

Greenspoon, J., "The Effect of Two Nonverbal Stimuli on the Frequency of Two Verbal Response Classes," *American Psychologist* 9:384 (1954).

Guttentag, O. E., "The Problem of Experimentation on Human Beings, II: The Physician's Point of View," *Science* 117:207–210 (1953).

Halpern, H. M., and L. N. Lesser, "Empathy in Infants, Adults and Psychotherapists," *Psychoanalysis and Psychoanalytic Review* 47:32–42 (1960).

158   BIBLIOGRAPHY

Herzberg, A., *Active Psychotherapy* (London: Research Books, Ltd., 1945).

Hesse, H., *Magister Ludi* (New York: Ungar, 1949).

Hildum, D. C., and R. W. Brown, "Verbal Reinforcement and Interviewer Bias," *Journal of Abnormal Social Psychology* 53:108–111 (1956).

Huxley, A., "Tyranny over the Mind," *Newsday*, May 31, 1958, pp. 1–24.

———— "Human Potentialities," in S. M. Farber and R. H. L. Wilson, eds., *Control of the Mind* (New York: McGraw-Hill, 1961).

Isaacs, W., J. Thomas, and I. Goldiamond, "Application of Operant Conditioning to Reinstate Verbal Behavior in Psychotics," *Journal of Speech and Hearing Disorders* 25:8–12 (1960).

Ivy, A. C., "The History and Ethics of the Use of Human Subjects in Medical Experiments," *Science* 108:1–5 (1948).

Josselyn, I. M., "Psychotherapy of Adolescents at the Level of Private Practice," in B. B. Balser, ed., *Psychotherapy of the Adolescent* (New York: International Universities Press, 1957).

Jung, C. G., *The Undiscovered Self* (Boston: Little Brown, 1958; paperback, New York, Mentor, 1959).

———— *Psychological Reflections: An Anthology from the writings of Carl G. Jung*, ed., J. Jacobi (New York: Pantheon, 1953; paperback, Harper Torchbook, 1961).

Kahler, E., *The Tower and the Abyss* (New York: Braziller, 1957).

Kelman, H., "Psychoanalysis and Science," *American Journal of Psychoanalysis* 13:38–58 (1953).

Kelman, H., "Psychoanalysis and Existentialism," in L. Saltzman and J. Masserman, eds., *Modern Concepts of Psychoanalysis* (New York: The Citadel Press, 1962).

King, G. F., S. G. Armitage, and J. R. Tilton, "An Operant-Interpersonal Therapeutic Approach to Schizophrenics of Extreme Pathology," *American Psychologist* 13:358 (1958).

Kobrin, S., "The Chicago Area Project—A 25-Year Assessment," in *Annals of the American Academy of Political and Social Science* 322:19–29 (1959).

Krasner, L., "Studies of the Conditioning of Verbal Behavior," *Psychological Bulletin* 55:148–170 (1958).

Kubie, L., "The Forgotten Man of Education," *Harvard Alumni Bulletin*, October 28, 1961, pp. 113–116.

Ladimer, I., "Human Experimentation: Medico-Legal Aspects," *New England Journal of Medicine* 257:18–24 (1957).

Lang, P. J., and A. D. Lazovik, "Experimental Desensitization of a Phobia," *Journal of Abnormal and Social Psychology* 66:519–525 (1963).

Langdon-Davies, J., *Man: The Known and the Unknown* (London:

Secker and Warburg, 1961). Available also under the title *On the Nature of Man* (paperback, New York, Mentor, 1961).

Lasagna, L., and J. M. von Felsinger, "The Volunteer Subject in Research," *Science* 120:359–361 (1954).

Lavin, N. I., J. G. Thorpe, J. C. Barker, C. B. Blakemore, and C. G. Conway, "Behavior Therapy in a Case of Transvestism," *Journal of Nervous and Mental Disease* 133:346–353 (1961).

Lazarus, A. A., "The Results of Behaviour Therapy in 126 Cases of Severe Neurosis," *Behaviour Research and Therapy* 1:69–79 (1963).

Leohr, F., *The Power of Prayer on Plants* (New York: Doubleday, 1959).

Levenson, E. A., "Jam Tomorrow—Jam Yesterday," *Etc.* 18:167–178 (1961).

Levine, M., and G. Spivack, "Incentive, Time Conception, and Self-Control in a Group of Emotionally Disturbed Boys," *Journal of Clinical Psychology* 15:110–113 (1959).

Martin, B., and D. Kubly, "Results of Treatment of Enuresis by a Conditioned Response Method," *Journal of Consulting Psychology* 19:71–73 (1955).

Martin, P. W., *Experiment in Depth* (London: Routledge, 1955).

May, R., "The Origins and Significance of the Existential Movement in Psychology," in R. May, E. Angel, and H. F. Ellenberger, eds., *Existence* (New York: Basic Books, 1958), pp. 3–36.

McClelland, D. C., *Personality* (New York: Dryden, 1951).

McCord, W., J. McCord, and I. K. Zola, *Origins of Crime* (New York: Columbia University Press, 1959).

McCorkle, L. W., and R. Korn, "Resocialization within Walls," *Annals of the American Academy of Political and Social Science* 293:88–98 (1954).

Miller, W. B., "The Impact of a Community Group Work Program on Delinquent Corner Groups," *Social Service Review* 31:390–406 (1957).

——— "Lower-Class Culture as a Generating Milieu of Gang Delinquency," *Journal of Social Issues* 14:5–19 (1958).

Mitscherlich, A., and F. Mielke, *Doctors of Infamy* (New York: Henry Schuman, 1949).

Moore, B. M., *Juvenile Delinquency: Research, Theory, and Comment* (Washington, D.C.: Association for Supervision and Curriculum Development of the National Education Association, 1958).

Morison, R. S., "Gradualness, Gradualness, Gradualness," *American Psychologist* 15:187–197 (1960).

Mullan, H., and I. A. Sanguiliano, "The Existential Matrix of Psychotherapy," *Psychoanalysis and Psychoanalytic Review* 47:87–99 (1960).

Murphy, F. S., M. M. Shirley, and H. L. Witmer, "The Incidence of Hidden Delinquency," *American Journal of Orthopsychiatry* 16:686–696 (1946).

Murphy, G., "New Vistas in Personality Research," *Personnel and Guidance Journal* 40:114–122 (1961).

Murray, E. J., "A Content-Analysis Method for Studying Psychotherapy," *Psychological Monographs*, 1956, p. 70.

New York City Youth Board, "Reaching the Group: An Analysis of Group Work Methods Used with Teen-agers," *Youth Board Monograph Number 4* (1956).

Nietzsche, F., *Philosophy*, W. H. Wright, ed. (New York: Modern Library, 1954).

Nuremberg Military Tribunals, *Trials of War Criminals* (Washington, D.C.: U.S. Government Printing Office, 1947), II, 181–184.

Parloff, M. B., "Some Factors Affecting the Quality of Therapeutic Relationships," *Journal of Abnormal and Social Psychology* 52:5–10 (1956).

———— "Therapist-Patient Relationships and Outcome of Psychotherapy," *Journal of Consulting Psychology* 25:29–38 (1961).

Peck, H. B., "Delinquency—A Laboratory for Public Health Psychiatry," *American Journal of Orthopsychiatry* 28:134–145 (1958).

Peltz, W., "Psychotherapy of Adolescents at Private Practice Plus School Practice Level," in B. H. Balzer, ed., *Psychotherapy of the Adolescent* (New York: International Universities Press, 1957), pp. 39–66.

Peters, H. N., and R. L. Jenkins, "Improvement of Chronic Schizophrenic Patients with Guided Problem-Solving Motivated by Hunger," *The Psychiatric Quarterly Supplement* (published semiannually by the New York State Department of Mental Hygiene, Utica, N.Y.), 28:84–101 (1954).

Quay, H., "The Effect of Verbal Reinforcement on the Recall of Early Memories," *Journal of Abnormal Social Psychology* 59:254–257 (1959).

Rachman, S., "Sexual Disorders and Behavior Therapy," *American Journal of Psychiatry* 118:235–240 (1961).

Reid, J. R., "Psychotherapy and Values," in L. Salzman and J. Masserman, eds., *Modern Concepts of Psychoanalysis* (New York: Citadel, 1962), pp. 21–43.

Reik, T., "New Ways in Psychoanalytic Technique," *International Journal of Psychoanalysis* 14:321–334 (1933).

Rogers, C. R., "The Necessary and Sufficient Conditions of Therapeutic Personality Change," *Journal of Consulting Psychology* 21:95–103 (1957).

———— "Cultural Evolution as Viewed by Psychologists," *Daedalus* 90:570–586 (1961).

Rogers, M. J., "Operant Conditioning in a Quasi-therapy Setting," *Journal of Abnormal Social Psychology* 60:247–252 (1960).

Rumney, J., and J. P. Murphy, *Probation and Social Adjustment* (New Brunswick, N.J.: Rutgers University Press, 1952).

Salter, A., "Learning and Unlearning Homosexuality," in *Conditioned Reflex Therapy* (New York: Farrar, Straus, 1949; paperback, Capricorn Books, 1961).

Schmideberg, M., "The Analytic Treatment of Major Criminals: Therapeutic Results and Technical Problems," in K. R. Eissler, ed., *Searchlights on Delinquency* (New York: International Universities Press, 1956), pp. 174–189.

Schwartz, E. E., "A Community Experience in the Measurement of Juvenile Delinquency," *National Probation and Parole Association Journal* 10:157–181 (1946).

Schwitzgebel, R., "A Review of Experimentation in Subception and Subliminal Stimulation," mimeographed (1958).

——— "A New Approach to Reducing Adolescent Crime," *Federal Probation*, March 1960, pp. 20–24.

——— "Reduction of Adolescent Crime by a Research Method," *Journal of Correctional Psychiatry and Social Therapy* 7:212–215 (1961).

——— "Delinquents with Tape Recorders," *New Society*, January 1963, pp. 14–16.

——— "Therapeutic Research," paper given at August 1963 meetings of the American Psychological Association in Philadelphia.

——— and T. H. Covey, "Experimental Interviewing of Youthful Offenders in a Church Setting," *Journal of Clinical Psychology* 19:487–488 (1963).

——— and D. A. Kolb, "Inducing Behaviour Change in Adolescent Delinquents," *Behaviour Research and Therapy* (1964). In press.

——— R. Schwitzgebel, W. N. Pahnke, and W. S. Hurd, "A Program for Research in Behavior Electronics," *Behavioral Science* (1964). In press.

Seeley, J. R., "Psychoanalysis: Model for Social Science," *Psychoanalysis and Psychoanalytic Review* 47:80–86 (1960).

Sellin, T., "Recidivism and Maturation," *National Probation and Parole Association Journal*, 1958, p. 4.

Shands, H. C., *Thinking and Psychotherapy: An Inquiry into the Processes of Communication* (Cambridge, Mass.: Harvard University Press, 1960).

Shannon, L. W., "The Problem of Competence to Help," *Federal Probation* 25:32–39 (1961).

Shapiro, L. N., M. Cohen, and W. Bugden, "Parole Violation and the Early Development of Internal Controls," *Archives of Criminal Psychodynamics*, Spring 1959, pp. 254–259.

Shimkin, M. D., "The Problem of Experimentation on Human Beings, I: The Research Worker's Point of View," *Science* 117:205–207 (1953).

Shoben, E. J., "Comments on 'Guidance as a Behavior Change,'" *Personnel and Guidance Journal* 39:560–562 (1961).

Siegel, S., *Nonparametric Statistics for the Behavioral Sciences* (New York: McGraw-Hill, 1956).

Skinner, B. F., *Cumulative Record* (New York: Appleton, 1959).

―――― and C. R. Rogers, "Some Issues Concerning the Control of Human Behavior," *Science* 124:1057–1066 (1956).

Slack, C. W., "Intensive Interpersonal Interviews with a Young Offender," mimeographed (April 1959).

―――― "Experimenter-Subject Psychotherapy: A New Method of Introducing Intensive Office Treatment for Unreachable Cases," *Mental Hygiene* 44:238–256 (1960).

―――― and D. Kantor, "Research Proposal: Experimenter-Subject Role in Total Treatment of Delinquents," mimeographed (March 1959).

―――― and R. Schwitzgebel, "Interpersonal Research," *Alabama Correctional Journal* 6:32–40 (1960).

Slavson, S. R., *The Fields of Group Psychotherapy* (New York: International Universities Press, 1956).

Staats, A. W., K. A. Minke, J. R. Finley, M. Wolf, and L. O. Brooks, "A Reinforcer System and Experimental Procedure for the Laboratory Study of Reading Acquisition," Technical Report no. 22, Contract NOUR–2794 (Psychological Processes in Communication), Office of Naval Research, September 1963, mimeographed.

Staats, C. K., A. W. Staats, and W. C. Heard, "Attitude Development and Ratio of Reinforcement," *Sociometry* 23:338–350 (1960).

State of New York, Division of Parole of the Executive Department, *Nineteenth Annual Report* (1949).

Strean, Herbert, "The Use of the Patient as Consultant," *Psychoanalysis and Psychoanalytic Review* 46:36–44 (1959).

―――― "Difficulties Met in the Treatment of Adolescents," *Psychoanalysis and Psychoanalytic Review* 48:69–80 (1961).

Strupp, H. H., "The Psychotherapeutic Contribution to the Treatment Process," *Behavioral Science* 3:34–67 (1958).

Sutherland, E. H., and D. R. Cressey, *Principles of Criminology,* 6 ed. (Philadelphia: Lippincott, 1960).

Taft, J. R., *Criminology,* 3 ed. (New York: Macmillan, 1956).

Taylor, R. E., "The Marquis de Sade and the First *Psychopathia Sexualis,*" in D. P. Geddes, ed. *An Analysis of the Kinsey Reports on Sexual Behavior in the Human Male and Female* (New York: Dutton, 1954; paperback, Mentor, 1954).

Teilhard de Chardin, P., *The Divine Milieu: An Essay on the Interior Life* (New York: Harper and Row, 1960).

United States Department of Justice, *Federal Prisons, 1959* (El Reno, Okla.: U.S. Reformatory, 1960).

Vold, G. B., "Does the Prison Reform?" *Annals of the American Academy of Political and Social Science* 293:42–50 (1954).

Walker, E. L., and R. W. Heyns, *An Anatomy for Conformity* (Englewood Cliffs, N.J.: Prentice-Hall, 1962).

Walker, H. M., and J. Lev, *Statistical Inference* (New York: Holt, Rinehart and Winston, 1953).

Watts, A., *Nature, Man, and Woman* (New York: Pantheon, 1958; paperback, Mentor, 1960).

Weigart, E., "Loneliness and Trust—Basic Factors of Human Existence," *Psychiatry* 23:121–131 (1960).

West, B., and F. Rafferty, "Initiating Therapy with Adolescents," *American Journal of Orthopsychiatry* 28:627–639 (1958).

Whyte, W. F., *Street-corner Society* (Chicago: University of Chicago Press, 1943).

Wilson, R. S., "Personality Patterns, Source Attractiveness, and Conformity," *Journal of Personality* 28:186–199 (1960).

Wolf Man, The, "How I Came into Analysis with Freud," *Journal of the American Psychoanalytic Association* 6:348–352 (1958).

Wolpe, J., "The Experimental Foundations of Some New Psychotherapeutic Methods," in A. J. Bachrach, ed., *Experimental Foundations of Clinical Psychology* (New York: Basic Books, 1962), pp. 554–575.

Wortis, J., *Fragments of an Analysis with Freud* (New York: Simon and Schuster, 1954).

Zuckerman, S. B., A. J. Barron, and B. B. Whittier, "A Follow-up Study of Minnesota State Reformatory Inmates: A Preliminary Report," *Journal of Criminal Law, Criminology, and Police Science* 43:622–636 (1953).

Index of Names

Index of Names

DATE DUE